This book is from

the kitchen library of

_____

_____

BY ART GINSBURG, MR. FOOD®

The Mr. Food® Cookbook, OOH IT'S SO GOOD!!™ (1990)

Mr. Food® Cooks Like Mama (1992)

Mr. Food® Cooks Chicken (1993)

Mr. Food® Cooks Pasta (1993)

Mr. Food® Makes Dessert (1993)

Mr. Food® Cooks Real American (1994)

Mr. Food®'s Favorite Cookies (1994)

Mr. Food®'s Quick and Easy Side Dishes (1995)

Mr. Food® Grills It All in a Snap (1995)

Mr. Food®'s Fun Kitchen Tips and Shortcuts (and Recipes, Too!) (1995)

Mr. Food®'s Old World Cooking Made Easy (1995)

"Help, Mr. Food®! Company's Coming!" (1995)

Mr. Food® Pizza 1-2-3 (1996)

Mr. Food® Meat Around the Table (1996)

Mr. Food® Simply Chocolate (1996)

Mr. Food® A Little Lighter (1996)

Mr. Food® From My Kitchen to Yours: Stories and Recipes from Home (1996)

Mr. Food® Easy Tex-Mex (1997)

Mr. Food® One Pot, One Meal (1997)

Mr. Food® Cool Cravings (1997)

Mr. Food®'s Italian Kitchen (1997)

Mr. Food®'s Simple Southern Favorites (1997)

A Mr. Food® Christmas: Homemade and Hassle-Free (1998)

Mr. Food® Cooking by the Calendar: Fifty-two Weeks of Year-Round Favorites (1999)

Mr. Food®'s Meals in Minutes (1999)

Mr. Food®'s Good Times, Good Food Cookbook (1999)

Mr. Food®'s Restaurant Favorites (1999)

Mr. Food®
A Little Lighter

Art Ginsburg
Mr. Food®

WILLIAM MORROW AND COMPANY, INC.

NEW YORK

Library of Congress Cataloging-in-Publication Data

Ginsburg, Art.
    Mr. Food® a little lighter / Art Ginsburg.
        p.   cm.
    Includes index.
    ISBN 0-688-13139-5
    1. Cookery.   2. Low-fat diet—Recipes.   I. Title.
TX714.G557   1996
641.5'638—dc20   96-17753
                                                                                        CIP

Printed in the United States of America

First Edition

        5   6   7   8   9   10

BOOK DESIGN BY MICHAEL MENDELSOHN OF MM DESIGN 2000, INC.

Dedicated to

You, my viewers and readers—

Live life to its fullest—
With a little *moderation* and a lot of

"OOH IT'S SO GOOD!!®"

Acknowledgments

You've asked for it, and here it is—a collection of my favorite foods made a little lighter. But just because the recipes are lighter doesn't mean that the work load was. As a matter of fact, this book was a perfect example of teamwork at its best. And what a team I have!

I need to start by tipping my chef's hat to the group of folks who spent countless hours with me in the kitchen. They were constantly testing, lightening, testing, adjusting, and retesting. Thanks to a real team leader, Patty Rosenthal; to Janice Bruce, who so expertly simplifies my recipes; to Cheryl Gerber, for bringing a touch of home to each recipe; and to Jo Ann Skelton, for adding yet another dimension to the team. And I thank Joe Peppi for making sure every version of each recipe was documented properly, and Laura Ratcliff for her administrative support.

Of course everyone in my office had a hand in making this book possible. Thanks to Steve, Chuck, Ethel, Tom, Beth, Chet, Marilyn, and Roy. And those not part of my office but definitely part of my team are my agent, Bill Adler, and Al Marchioni, Zachary Schisgal, Richard Aquan, Kim Yorio, Deborah Weiss Geline, and my other friends at William Morrow. My appreciation also extends to Michael Mendelsohn and Philip Scheuer, who capture my feelings through their designs and illustrations.

Once again, I couldn't have done this without Howard Rosenthal and Caryl Ginsburg Fantel. I don't know how to thank them adequately for helping me lighten up and put everything together for you.

As always, I must thank you, my viewers and readers, for supporting me, for challenging me, and for sharing your thoughts and recipe suggestions. You are why I love what I do!

There have been so many individuals, food councils, and organizations that have generously shared information and recipe ideas with me. I thank you all, including:

Badia Spices, Inc.
Borden
Comstock Foods
Dairy Management Inc.
Jana Brands, makers of frozen seafood products
The National Beef Council and Meat Marketing Board
National Cancer Institute
Lynda O'Neill
Tryson House®, makers of flavor mists
United States Department of Agriculture
Walnut Marketing Board

Contents

Introduction

For years I've been sharing so much with you—recipes, tips, and kitchen shortcuts. But lately I've gotten a lot more requests for ways to lighten up without sacrificing taste. Now don't get me wrong—I'm not talking about strict diets or food fads, because I know, and so do you, that most people never stick to diets that are extreme. My approach with this book is one that most people can easily live with . . . and it's really what my philosophy has been all along—that **moderation** is the key.

Yup, except for those people who are under a physician's care or on a restricted diet, I believe that we can cut down by simply adjusting our eating habits to watch what and how much we eat—while still enjoying food. And since you've asked me to address so many types of food restrictions, I've tried to do just that in this book.

These recipes are not fat-free, calorie-free, or sodium-free. They're just lighter, more moderate versions of the traditional recipes. In some of these recipes I've *reduced* the fat, in some I've *reduced* the sugar, in others the salt. Some recipes use fresh eggs, others use egg substitute. Yet one thing I have refused to give up is taste. So don't worry! By making the recipes this way *and* by serving smaller portions than you may be used to, you'll be able to cut back while still being more than satisfied.

If you want to do your own substitutions, that's fine. Don't forget to make these *your* recipes. But keep in mind that when you completely remove one or two ingredients, you may want to put something else in their place. That's why these recipes were so carefully put together. For example, removing fat often reduces flavor and makes food drier and tougher. Depending on the food you're working with, you may want to compensate for the reduction of fat. In meat and poultry dishes you could add more cooking liquids, such as water, defatted broth, and/or wine. And, as you'll see in a few of the dark-colored bread and dessert recipes here, applesauce and prune purée make good baking substitutes for oil and butter. Of course, removing salt from your cooking doesn't have to be a problem at all. We have so many great herb and spice choices available to us that I'm sure you'll be thrilled at the new taste adventures possible when you use one or a few of them—or even just black pepper—in place of all or some of the salt in recipes.

There are lots of products available that are already low in fat, sugar, sodium, cholesterol . . . you name it! Why, on the cover of this book I show turkey sausage (it makes up the letter G in the title!). It's a great option for people who enjoy sausage flavor and texture but need to do it with less fat. We're so lucky that food manufacturers are making changes and giving us so many options!

You know, what we eat really starts at the grocery store, so on pages xvii to xxiv I discuss how to shop and what to look for, including a section on how to read nutrition labels (page xxiii). Of course, if you're reading this, the chance is good that you want to make some lifestyle changes, so I've got some really helpful tips for you in Get Ready, Get Set, Go Lighter! (page xv) and in the Notes from **Mr. Food°** (page xxvii). In the section Eating Out, Eating Right (page xxv), I get to share moderation tricks that I use when I eat out. And wait until you see what's in store for you at the beginning of each chapter—loads of tips and shortcuts for making moderation work for you.

Now moderation refers not only to *what* we eat, but *how much* we eat. So watch those portion sizes! Yes, I think it's fine to eat meat if you're watching yourself, but it's best to use the leanest cuts possible, trim excess fat before and after cooking, *and* consume

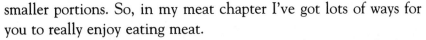

smaller portions. So, in my meat chapter I've got lots of ways for you to really enjoy eating meat.

I've also come up with all-new ways to enjoy eating chicken, turkey, fish, and other seafood. Just thumb through the choices and I know your mouth will be watering.

Vegetables and fruit have always been wonderful choices for us, so I encourage eating lots of those with all the selections I've got for you in my chapters of Salads and Dressings, Side Dishes, and even Meatless Main Dishes. And there are fabulous offerings in T.V. Snacks, Appetizers, Soups, and Breads and Muffins.

With desserts, I always said that one piece of cake has half the calories (and everything else) of two pieces. So, even though my desserts are wonderfully lighter than ever before, if you're trying to cut your fat, calorie, and sugar intake, it's still better to eat less overall.

When I was testing these recipes and trying them out on my staff, my family, and anyone who happened to stop by, the response was overwhelming! First, they really loved the food. Then, when I told them it was for my *Lighter* book, they couldn't believe that what they had just eaten was "lighter." I know you're going to be surprised, too.

Now you're ready to get yourself and your family on the path toward tasty, lighter eating.

> Put the guilt on the back burner,
> roll up your sleeves,
> and begin to cook up a lighter,
> tasty-as-ever

"OOH IT'S SO GOOD!!®"

Get Ready, Get Set, Go Lighter!

Cooking a little lighter doesn't mean you have to revamp your kitchen. All you have to do is follow a few basic steps and you'll be ready to enjoy a healthier "OOH IT'S SO GOOD!!®"

- Select the proper cooking techniques to help you reduce fat—baking, steaming, poaching, broiling, and grilling are good alternatives to frying and sautéing.
- Try to use heavy nonstick pots and pans. That'll mean that your cooking requires less fat to keep food from sticking.
- Replace regular full-fat dairy products, packaged and canned foods, and prepared frozen meals with reduced-fat, low-fat, or fat-free alternatives, such as low-fat milk or evaporated skim milk instead of heavy cream, etc.
- Move toward reduced-fat condiments like salsa, mustard, and prepared horseradish or use lighter versions or smaller amounts of your other favorites.
- When adding butter or oil, do so right before serving so it flavors your food instead of being completely absorbed into the food. Again, use these in moderation.
- Eggs can still be part of your diet, if used in moderation. There are also great egg substitutes available in the refrigerated section of the supermarket (usually right near the eggs). Two egg whites equal one whole egg.
- Add a splash of vinegar or citrus juice—lemon, lime, or orange—to dressings, marinades, vegetables, poultry, almost anything—to wake up your taste buds.
- Strong-flavored cheeses such as Parmesan, Romano, and blue

cheese can be added sparingly to dishes to enhance flavoring. And a little goes a long way!

As I said in my Introduction, if you want to indulge yourself with a food high in fat, calories, or something else you're trying to stay away from, decide that you're going to treat yourself *just a bit* and *exercise moderation*.

It's important not only *what* you eat, but *how* you eat. So follow a few basic common-sense eating habits:

- Eat regularly scheduled meals and limit eating between meals. There are two rules of thumb on this: Eat three scheduled meals a day and limit eating between meals OR eat five to six light meals throughout the day. But don't do both, and *never* stuff yourself!
- Try not to eat within two hours of bedtime.
- Watch portion sizes! Smaller portions mean fewer calories, so serve yourself only as much food as you think you'll eat. It's okay to leave some on your plate, too.

Grocery Shopping Tips

Hate grocery shopping?? You're not alone! Yes, grocery shopping takes time. We have to check our fridge and cabinets, then make our lists, check for coupons, go to the store and choose our items, then unpack and put them away when we get home. But it's something that's gotta be done—so here's my "shopping cart" of tips to make it as easy as possible to save time and money at the store:

- It's easier to eat lighter if you have the items you want on hand. So before heading to the store, make a list. Even if you're sure you know what you need, you'll do better if you make yourself a list. And if your gang is like mine and always has something to say about what you buy, then get them involved in making the list, too. That way they can have their say ahead of time *and* give you more of a chance to please everybody!

- Try to shop at off-peak hours. Peak hours are after work (just before dinner) and weekend mornings, so avoid those times. Instead, try early on weekday mornings, or in the evening. You'll save a bunch of time just by doing that. (And wouldn't you rather spend your shopping time picking the best tomatoes instead of picking the

best route around all the other shopping carts?! You might even think of it as exercise, if you move quickly around the store.)

- Is it best to shop on a full stomach or an empty stomach? Shopping experts disagree on this point. If you shop on an empty stomach, you're more apt to buy on impulse, and usually that means food that looks good but isn't necessarily the smartest purchase. After all, it's no fun to go through the aisles with your stomach growling! And you may be in too much of a hurry to pick up everything you really need. But if you shop on a full stomach, things may not be as appealing to you and you *still* may not get everything you need. On the other hand, you shop more practically (that's where the all-important list comes in really handy). I know you can't always choose the best time to shop, so if you have to do it before a meal, I suggest having a light snack before you go.

- Clipping coupons does you no good if you forget to take them shopping with you! Have an organizer envelope or box to keep coupons together by product type so that you can save time and money—but only if they're for products that you're going to use. Manufacturers are offering coupons for light versions of old standby products; if you come across these, it might be a good time to check out some new products. (Always remember to check coupon expiration dates.)

- Watch weekly store advertisements for the sales that usually begin on Thursdays. That's when the supplies of the special items are plentiful. Many of these on-sale items are considered "loss leaders" by the stores. That means that the stores reduce their prices on certain popular items to entice you to shop there. Take advantage of these sales whenever possible, but don't get trapped into buying nonsale items that you know are overpriced on that same shopping trip. And even though items may be offered at good prices, don't stop reading the labels, especially if you're trying to eat lighter.

- Check your list carefully as you shop, checking off items and making notes if you need to.
- Should you buy store brands instead of national brands? It's up to you. Store brands are usually priced better and are often processed and packaged by the same companies that process and package the national brands. There are more and more stores coming out with their own light items, too. But you should always check the labels and compare the individual items. You won't get good value from a product if your family won't eat or use it!
- Don't forget to check the high and low shelves in the supermarket. Often the best bargains are there, not at eye level. Many of the less-popular light items are on these shelves, too, so look, look, look!
- Keep in mind the price difference between convenience foods and homemade foods, including traditional favorites and lighter versions. You're the specialist on what your family likes and what you have time for. Sometimes it ends up being less expensive to go with convenience and, say, buy one bag of mixed salad greens instead of separate types of fresh greens.

Here's a list of other things to remember:

- Don't buy dented cans or any products with cracked seals.
- Check label dates. The dates listed are generally the last date that the food can be sold, not the last date it can be eaten.
- Fruit and vegetables are an important part of eating right, so have lots of them on hand. Try to stick to the five-a-day rule that recommends having at least five servings a day of fruit and vegetables. Carefully check produce for bruises and soft spots. Handpicking each of your items from the produce counters helps to ensure that you buy high-quality items. An example is oranges—if you buy a large bag of them, you can't examine each

one the way you can if you pick them out individually. Bulk packages are usually priced better, but if you end up buying items that you can't eat . . . there go your savings!

- Buy meat, poultry, and fish as fresh as possible, and be sure the item you choose is really what you want and how you want it. See my tips at the beginning of the meat and fish chapters (pages 143 to 144 and 175 to 176). Don't buy ground turkey parts if you really want ground turkey breast, etc. Ask the butcher for suggestions. He's the pro and can probably save you some money and calories.
- Don't buy frozen foods that look as if they've been thawed and refrozen. Also, ask the check-out person to pack the frozen items in plastic bags or freezer bags so they won't thaw or make a mess before you get them home. It might be a good idea to keep an inexpensive cooler in the car for getting these things home.
- Buy just enough baked goods for a few days. See my tips at the beginning of the bread and dessert chapters (pages 257 and 279 to 280). Don't buy a week's worth at a time, because, chances are, they won't stay fresh—or you'll eat them just because they're there. It's better to pick up select items throughout the week. They'll be fresher and you'll be helping your willpower, too.

Food Labels Made Easy

For a while, food manufacturers developed their own random names for "light" food products. There was no consistency from one brand to the next, or one type of food to the next. But now that the United States Department of Agriculture regulates what companies can refer to as "light," "reduced-fat," etc., we can be more confident in these claims—though we should still read our food labels completely and carefully. The chart below explains the current guidelines for using these various terms.

Package Wording	Definition
Reduced-fat or less fat	The product has a minimum of 25 percent less fat per serving than the traditional version of the food.
Low-fat	The product has no more than 3 grams of fat per serving.
Saturated fat-free	The product has less than 0.5 gram of saturated fat per serving.
Fat-free	The product contains less than 0.5 gram of fat per serving.
Light	The product has 50 percent less fat OR ⅓ fewer calories per serving than the traditional version of the food.
Reduced-sodium or reduced-salt	The product contains 25 percent less sodium per serving than the traditional version of the food.

Package Wording	Definition
Reduced-cholesterol	The product contains at least 25 percent less cholesterol and 2 grams or less of saturated fat per serving than the traditional version of the food.
Cholesterol-free	The product contains less than 2 milligrams of cholesterol and 2 grams or less of saturated fat per serving.

Once you get past the name of a product and its claims of being lighter in one or more ingredients, there's more to examine. Food packaging may contain health claims that explain the value of the product. For example, a food high in fiber and low in saturated fat could be claimed to reduce cholesterol levels and, therefore, a person's risk of heart disease if he consumes that product. I can't stress enough that you should read food labels completely and carefully; and, if you have any questions about particular foods, ask your physician.

Every time you pick a food item off the supermarket shelf, you should see a nutrition label, called Nutrition Facts, somewhere on the package. And you shouldn't have to look too hard for it, either, because the government regulates the size of the labels. It also has strict guidelines regarding the information that is contained in these labels. This means that we can count on them being large and clear enough to read and understand easily. Okay, the reading part isn't usually a problem. But what about the understanding part?

Here's a sample nutritional fact label and an explanation of what those numbers mean to us:

Nutrition Facts			
Serving Size ½ cup (114g)			
Servings per Container 4			
Amount per Serving			
Calories 90		Calories from Fat 30	
		% Daily Value*	
Total Fat 3g		5%	
Saturated Fat 0g		0%	
Cholesterol 0mg		0%	
Sodium 300mg		13%	
Total Carbohydrate 13g		4%	
Dietary Fiber 3g		12%	
Sugars 3g			
Protein 3g			
Vitamin A 80%	•	Vitamin C 60%	
Calcium 4%	•	Iron 4%	

*Percent Daily Values are based on a 2,000 calorie diet. Your daily values may be higher or lower depending on your calorie needs.

	Calories:	2,000	2,500
Total Fat	Less than	65g	80g
Sat Fat	Less than	20g	25g
Cholesterol	Less than	300mg	300mg
Sodium	Less than	2,400mg	2,400mg
Total Carbohydrate		300g	375g
Fiber		25g	30g

Calories per gram:
Fat 9   •   Carbohydrate 4   •   Protein 4

1. Serving Size—This is what is considered to be standard for the item, and you may find that your serving size fluctuates quite a bit by how small or large a serving you and your family eat of a particular item.
2. Servings per Container—Again, the servings are just a guideline of what is considered average.
3. To most of us, the most important information is the amount of fat, cholesterol, sodium, carbohydrates, and nutrients contained in the food. That's why they're listed not only in milligrams, but also as a percentage of an average person's daily allotment, based on a daily 2,000-calorie diet. Your own Daily Values for these items may be higher or lower, depending on your level of activity.

4. Only two vitamins, A and C, and two minerals, calcium and iron, are required listings on food labels. Food companies may voluntarily list others, though.

5. Some labels list the approximate number of calories in a gram of fat, carbohydrate, and protein.

Since the format of and information contained on food labels is supposed to be consistent from product to product and brand to brand, you can do your own comparisons and balance your food choices. Few foods provide 100 percent of a single nutrient, so the percentage values on the packages can help us focus our diets and make knowledgeable nutrition choices. As always, if you'd like further information on how to shape your own diet, the best place to start is with your physician.

Eating Out, Eating Right

Sure, we like to cook at home, but every now and then we like to eat out at our favorite restaurant. And eating out doesn't have to mean we break our good eating habits from home. Since I make so many appearances around the country, I've come up with some tips to help cut down on fat and calories:

- Watch what you drink! Drink water, brewed iced tea, unsweetened sparkling water, or *natural* fruit juices rather than soft drinks, sugar-laden fruit juices, or milk shakes. A slice of fresh lemon or lime will add a zip to your water or iced tea, too.
- Don't be tempted by all the bread and rolls. If you fill up early, you won't enjoy the right foods later in the meal. And if you use butter, go easy on it.
- Eat just as you would at home. Don't order more than you would normally eat. If you have the option, order a small portion or cut.
- Instead of ordering a full meal, try ordering a salad and then an appetizer as your entrée.
- Ask if your meal can be grilled, poached, or steamed instead of deep-fried or sautéed.
- Choose the right side dishes—like maybe steamed vegetables instead of French fries, or a plain baked potato rather than one served with butter and/or sour cream.
- Ask for dressings, sauces, and condiments on the side so that you can control the desired amounts. Of course, you can always request reduced-fat and/or reduced-calorie versions.
- You don't have to skip dessert. Just order fresh fruit, fruit ices, frozen yogurt, or my favorite—share a dessert with a friend or two.

Notes from **Mr. Food**®

Lighten Up ... with Food Sprays

Throughout this book, and in my other cookbooks, I frequently mention nonstick vegetable and baking sprays and recommend using them to coat pans before placing food in or on them. Here's why—these sprays and mists are easy to use and, used as directed, they add no measurable amount of fat to our food; and now they're even available in nonaerosol *and* in flavored varieties! The flavored sprays and mists are super ways to add a touch of taste, either before or after cooking foods, without adding lots of fat and calories.

Serving Sizes

I normally like to serve generous-sized portions, but I cut down a bit when I listed the number of servings from each of these recipes. Yes, appetites do vary, but if you and your family are trying to cut down, help each other by serving smaller portions or by putting on your plates only what you think you'll eat. You can even serve food on smaller plates. It helps makes portions look fuller when you're cutting down. This all makes sense . . . you'll see!

Packaged Foods

Packaged food sizes may vary by brand. Generally, the sizes indicated in these recipes are average sizes. If you can't find the exact package size listed in the ingredients, whatever package is closest in size will usually do the trick. And, as I mention throughout the book, look for foods that are truly lighter (get help from Food Labels Made Easy, page xxi). Read and understand the labels. It's an easy way to start lightening up, and every product brand may vary, so try different ones until you're satisfied.

T.V. Snacks

You finally get to plop yourself down on the couch, grab the remote control, and relax in front of the T.V. But after a few minutes your stomach growls and you know it's happening . . . the munchies have set in! Do you think there's a direct relationship between watching television and our stomachs?

Over the years I've found that certain foods seem to taste and handle better than others for eating in front of the T.V. And I've also realized through my own experience that these super munchies can add loads of calories and fat to our diets if we don't use moderation. So now I'll share what I've learned to help you satisfy those persistent munchies:

- If you're going to eat while sitting on a couch or in an easy chair, be sure to sit upright.
- Stick to foods that are easy to eat and aren't too messy. Dips, chips, and spreads are okay as long as the dips aren't too thin and drippy. (And how 'bout using small plates to make eating easier and keep furniture clean?!)
- If you're going to nibble, it's a great way to get some of your recommended five-a-day servings of fruit and vegetables. Fresh-cut vegetables, with or without a light dip, and fresh whole or cut fruit are your best choices. It's great to have these on hand, stored on the top shelf of the fridge, because the more accessible they are, the better off we'll be. (Accessibility is the biggest reason why too often we simply reach for the soda and chips.)
- Pay attention to the nutrition labels on your snack foods—they tell you a lot. Check my section on nutrition labels, page xxi.

Today's snack manufacturers are giving us more and better options to choose from. Baked packaged snacks are better than fried ones—and better yet are homemade Garlic Pita Crisps (page 8).

- Air-popped popcorn is a great treat. You can even add a touch of butter to moisten and flavor it—but remember: Be moderate. A little goes a long way.
- Make dips with reduced-fat ingredients whenever possible. Use reduced-fat mayonnaise, sour cream, cream cheese, and yogurt as dip bases. They'll really make a difference.
- Keep salsa on hand. It's available in strengths from mild to hot, and in forms from spreadable to chunky. There's the most common type, which is the spicy tomato-based type, and then there are onion- and even fruit-based ones. A good alternative to creamy dips, salsa has lots of flavor without lots of fat and calories.
- A general rule is to eat regularly scheduled meals to reduce the temptation to nibble between them.
- Try not to eat within two hours of bedtime. Your digestive system needs a chance to digest food before you go to sleep.

T.V. Snacks

Tortilla Crisps

64 crisps

Bet you didn't know you could make your own tortilla chips! Well, you can. And this way, not only do you get to control the amount of fat in them, but you can bake them when you want them, for that "fresh from the oven" flavor.

Eight 10-inch flour tortillas   Nonstick vegetable spray

Preheat the oven to 425°F. Coat a rimmed baking sheet with non-stick vegetable spray. Place 2 tortillas on a cutting board and coat both sides of each tortilla with the spray. Cut each tortilla into 8 wedges. Place on the baking sheet and bake for 6 to 8 minutes, or until golden. Repeat with the remaining tortillas. Allow to cool, then store in an airtight container until ready to use.

NOTE: These are a perfect go-along for Garden-Style Salsa Salad (page 69). I can't wait till you taste that completely delicious home-made flavor.

Garlic Pita Crisps

96 triangles

Looking for a great all-around snack? Stop right here, 'cause you can eat these plain or with dips, and you can make them any flavor you want simply by changing the spices.

Six 6-inch pita breads
2 tablespoons garlic powder

1½ teaspoons salt
Nonstick vegetable spray

Preheat the oven to 350°F. Cut each pita into 8 equal-sized wedges. Separate each wedge into 2 pieces. In a large resealable plastic storage bag, combine the garlic powder and salt. Coat both sides of the pita wedges lightly with nonstick vegetable spray, then place about ¼ of the wedges in the plastic bag and shake until evenly coated. Place the wedges in a single layer on a large rimmed baking sheet. Repeat with the remaining wedges and additional baking sheets. Bake for 15 minutes, or until golden brown and crisp. Allow to cool. Serve immediately, or store in an airtight container until ready to use.

NOTE: For variety, use onion powder or dried Italian seasoning instead of garlic powder. These are super with Today's Hummus (page 13)!

Homemade Soft Pretzels

10 pretzels

Most of today's shopping malls have shops or kiosks that sell warm fresh-baked pretzels. Now you can make and enjoy them right from your own oven! (Oh—I'm sure you can find some other reason to go to the mall!)

1 package (10 to 11 ounces) refrigerated pizza crust
1 egg white

1 tablespoon water
1 teaspoon coarse (kosher) salt

Preheat the oven to 350°F. On a lightly floured countertop, roll the dough into a 10" × 16" rectangle. Cut the dough lengthwise into ten 1-inch-wide strips. Form each strip into a pretzel shape and place on a large rimmed baking sheet that has been coated with nonstick vegetable spray. In a small bowl, combine the egg white and water; beat slightly, then brush the mixture over the pretzel tops and sprinkle with the salt. Bake for 15 to 17 minutes, or until golden. Serve warm.

NOTE: Canned refrigerated pizza crust is found in the supermarket refrigerator section along with the doughs and biscuits. For a little variety, try topping these with onion salt or garlic salt instead of coarse salt.

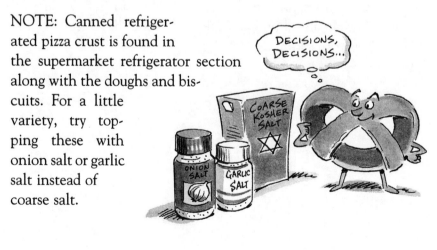

Mix-'Em-Up Snack Mix

About 8 cups

You won't be able to keep up with the demand for this crunchy snack mix with a spicy bite.

2 cups oven-toasted corn cereal
2 cups oven-toasted rice cereal
2 cups oven-toasted wheat cereal
2 cups miniature pretzel twists
¼ cup Worcestershire sauce

3 tablespoons canola or
    vegetable oil
1 teaspoon onion powder
1 teaspoon garlic powder
½ teaspoon cayenne pepper

Preheat the oven to 300°F. In a large bowl, combine the cereals and pretzels. In a small bowl, combine the remaining ingredients; mix well. Pour the seasoning mixture over the cereal mixture and toss until thoroughly coated. Spread the mixture on 2 rimmed baking sheets and bake for 45 minutes, stirring every 15 minutes. Remove from the oven and cool completely. Store in an airtight container until ready to use.

NOTE: Oven-toasted cereals are available in many different brands. And go ahead and add raisins or other dried fruit if you'd like—it's *your* snack mix!

Italian-Style Nachos

6 to 8 servings

Okay, so when you think of Italian food you don't think of nachos. Well, why not change that? Tortilla chips make a great base for pizza-like nachos—and they're ready in no time.

1 bag (8 ounces) tortilla chips
1 cup light spaghetti sauce
1 can (4 ounces) mushroom
    pieces and stems, drained and
    patted dry

½ teaspoon crushed red pepper
½ cup (2 ounces) shredded part-
    skim mozzarella cheese

Preheat the oven to 425°F. Place the tortilla chips on a 12-inch pizza pan or a large rimmed baking sheet. Pour the spaghetti sauce evenly over the chips, then scatter the mushroom pieces over the sauce. Sprinkle with the crushed red pepper, then the cheese. Bake for 4 to 6 minutes, or until the cheese has melted. Serve immediately.

NOTE: For a little added spice, chop some peperoncini and sprinkle them over the top before baking.

Black Bean Dip

About 4 cups

The pinto bean used to be considered the king for bean dips, but black beans have been gaining popularity lately. Once you taste this dip, you'll see why!

2 cans (16 ounces each) black beans, rinsed and drained, divided

1 jar (8 ounces) picante sauce, divided

1 teaspoon vegetable oil

1 medium-sized onion, finely chopped

1 medium-sized red bell pepper, finely chopped

3 garlic cloves, minced

1 tablespoon dried cilantro

2 teaspoons ground cumin

¾ teaspoon salt

½ cup (2 ounces) shredded Cheddar cheese

1 medium-sized tomato, chopped

In a blender or a food processor that has been fitted with its steel cutting blade, combine 1 can beans and ¼ cup picante sauce; blend or process until smooth. Heat the oil in a large nonstick skillet over medium heat and sauté the onion, pepper, and garlic for 5 to 7 minutes, or until the onion is tender. Add the puréed bean mixture, the cilantro, cumin, salt, and the remaining whole beans and pi-cante sauce; mix well. Bring to a boil, then reduce the heat to low and simmer for 5 minutes, stirring frequently. Pour the dip into a shallow serving dish and top with the cheese and tomato.

NOTE: Serve this with Tortilla Crisps (page 7) or your favorite low-fat tortilla chips.

Today's Hummus

About 4 cups

I have to share a favorite of mine from my *Old World* cookbook. It's so easy! And now this favorite of yesteryear is lighter in every way except taste. You'll see. . . .

2 cans (15 to 19 ounces each) garbanzo beans (chick peas), drained and ⅓ cup of the liquid reserved
3 garlic cloves, minced

¼ cup fresh lemon juice (juice of 2 to 3 lemons)
3 tablespoons olive oil
1 teaspoon ground cumin
1½ teaspoons salt

Combine all the ingredients in a food processor that has been fitted with its steel cutting blade. Process until the mixture is smooth and creamy and no lumps remain, scraping down the sides of the bowl as needed. Serve immediately, or cover and chill until ready to use.

NOTE: Serve with pita bread triangles. And if your pitas are a bit dry, try brushing them with a bit of olive oil and heating them in a warm oven for 5 minutes just before serving.

Roasted Pepper Dip

About 2 cups

Roasted peppers are certainly popular today. And when they're made into a dip, they give us a before-meal treat packed with flavor but not calories.

1 jar (7 ounces) roasted red peppers, drained, patted dry, and finely chopped (about ½ cup)

1 container (16 ounces) reduced-fat sour cream
1 teaspoon minced garlic
1 teaspoon salt

In a medium-sized bowl, with an electric beater on medium speed, beat all the ingredients until thoroughly blended. Serve immediately, or store in the refrigerator in an airtight container until ready to use.

NOTE: Serve with assorted fresh-cut vegetables for dipping. To roast your own peppers, cut 3 medium-sized bell peppers (any color) into 1-inch strips. In a medium-sized bowl, combine 2 tablespoons olive oil and ¼ teaspoon each of garlic powder, onion powder, salt, and black pepper. Add the pepper strips and toss to coat, then place in a 9" × 13" baking dish. In a preheated 450°F. oven, bake for 20 to 25 minutes, or until the peppers are fork-tender.

Hot Artichoke Spread

About 4 cups

This is packed with super flavor, so no one will have to know you made it "light" by using light mayonnaise!

1 cup light mayonnaise
2 cans (14 ounces each) water-
    packed artichoke hearts,
    drained

Dash of hot pepper sauce
1 garlic clove, minced
1 teaspoon lemon juice
½ cup grated Parmesan cheese

Preheat the oven to 350°F. Place all the ingredients in a food processor that has been fitted with its steel cutting blade and process until smooth. Pour the mixture into a 7" × 11" baking dish that has been coated with nonstick vegetable spray and bake for 30 minutes, or until lightly browned.

NOTE: Serve with whole wheat crackers.

Amaretto Fruit Dip

About 1½ cups

Make T.V. time a little more special by serving something a bit out of the ordinary.

1 package (8 ounces) reduced-fat cream cheese, softened
1 jar (7 ounces) marshmallow creme

2 tablespoons amaretto or almond extract

Place all the ingredients in a medium-sized bowl; beat with an electric beater on medium speed until well blended. Cover and chill until ready to serve.

NOTE: Serve with whole fresh strawberries, slices of apples, peaches, or pears, or any of your favorite fruits.

Strawberry Cream Dip

About 1 ½ cups

For a quick and healthy snack, nothing fits the bill like fresh fruit. And when you cut it up and serve it with this dip, nobody can resist it.

1 package (8 ounces) reduced-fat cream cheese, softened

½ cup low-fat vanilla yogurt
½ cup strawberry jam

In a medium-sized bowl, with an electric beater on medium speed, beat the cream cheese until creamy. Add the yogurt and strawberry jam and continue beating until smooth. Cover and chill for at least 1 hour, or until ready to serve.

NOTE: Serve this with fresh-cut chunks of cantaloupe, honeydew, or pineapple, apple slices, and whole strawberries . . . it all works! And you can also substitute your favorite flavor of jam or preserves for the strawberry jam.

Chip Dip

About 1 ½ cups

Here's an age-old classic—onion dip—but with a lot less fat. This one will let you dip again and again.

1 can (15 to 19 ounces) garbanzo
    beans (chick peas), drained
    and ½ cup liquid reserved
½ cup reduced-fat sour cream

1 envelope (1 ounce) onion
    soup mix
1 tablespoon chopped fresh
    parsley

In a blender or a food processor that has been fitted with its steel cutting blade, purée the garbanzo beans and the reserved ½ cup liquid until smooth and creamy. In a medium-sized bowl, combine the remaining ingredients. Add the puréed garbanzo beans and mix well with a spoon. Store in the refrigerator in an airtight container until ready to use.

NOTE: Serve with Garlic Pita Crisps (page 8) as an alternative to your favorite chips. And if you don't have fresh parsley on hand, go ahead and use 1 teaspoon dried parsley flakes instead.

Appetizers

Once in a while it's okay to fancy up a meal by starting off with an appetizer. Or make several appetizers to have as a light meal when the gang drops by. But don't overdo the choices and serving sizes before a meal. You don't want your guests to fill up on appetizers and then feel pressured to eat a whole main course besides. Here are a few suggestions for lightening up your appetizers:

- Always have a combination of fresh-cut veggies like celery, carrots, broccoli and cauliflower florets, and bell peppers as an available option. You can put them out plain, with salsa, or with one of the dressings on pages 93 to 98.
- Stay away from fried appetizers. "Oven-fried" or baked finger foods are better options.
- Traditional chicken wings are fun, but the skin contains about 50 percent of the fat in chicken. Create the same taste by using boneless and skinless chicken tenders. See Buffalo Chicken Tenders (page 30).
- Extend some of your richer favorites. For example, take shrimp, which is relatively high in cholesterol. If you're allowed to have it once in a while, then just 1 or 2 served on a bed of shredded lettuce with a dollop of cocktail sauce makes a great appetizer. Not only is it half the cholesterol of an average portion, but it's half the cost, too!

Appetizers

Party Stuffed Mushrooms

12 to 15 mushrooms

In the past, I've liked stuffing mushrooms with sausage. But using fresh mushrooms in the stuffing instead helps make a lighter version of this old-time favorite.

1 pound large fresh mushrooms
¼ cup water
¼ cup dry bread crumbs

¼ teaspoon onion powder
¼ teaspoon salt
⅛ teaspoon black pepper

Preheat the oven to 350°F. Gently clean the mushrooms by rubbing with a damp cloth. Remove the stems from ¾ pound of the mushrooms; set aside the caps. Finely chop the stems and the remaining ¼ pound whole mushrooms. Place in a large skillet, add the water, and cook over medium heat for 4 to 5 minutes, until softened. Remove from the heat and add the remaining ingredients; mix well. Using a teaspoon, stuff the mushroom caps with the mixture. Place on an ungreased rimmed baking sheet and bake for 10 minutes, or until warmed through.

Turkey Stuffing Meatballs

About 4 dozen meatballs

Any time you're longing for the tastes of your favorite holiday dinner, try these. It's easy to get your turkey, stuffing, and cranberry sauce all rolled into one!

1 bag (8 ounces) herb-seasoned
    stuffing cubes
1 egg white
1 tablespoon ground sage
1 cup hot water

1 pound ground turkey breast
1 can (16 ounces) jellied
    cranberry sauce
½ cup sugar

Preheat the oven to 400°F. In a large bowl, combine the stuffing, egg white, and sage; mix well. Slowly add the hot water; mix well. Add the ground turkey; mix well. Roll into 1-inch balls and place the meatballs on rimmed baking sheets that have been coated with nonstick vegetable spray. Bake for 20 to 25 minutes, or until cooked through, turning halfway through the baking. Meanwhile, in a small saucepan, combine the cranberry sauce and sugar over low heat, stirring occasionally until the sugar melts. Place in a bowl and serve with the meatballs.

NOTE: Make sure you use ground turkey breast, which typically has much less fat than regular ground turkey (which is ground from a combination of turkey parts).

Chicken on a Stick

16 to 20 skewers

Who said eating lighter is boring? No way! This chicken has the saucy combination of cayenne pepper and brown sugar—a taste sensation that'll keep you and your gang coming back for more.

Sixteen to twenty 6- to 8-inch wooden or metal skewers
4 boneless, skinless chicken breast halves, cut into 1-inch strips

1 cup firmly packed light brown sugar
4 teaspoons lemon juice
1 teaspoon salt
½ teaspoon cayenne pepper

Preheat the oven to 350°F. If using wooden skewers, soak them in water for 15 to 20 minutes. Thread 1 chicken strip onto each skewer. In a medium-sized bowl, combine the remaining ingredients; mix well. Coat the chicken with the mixture and place on a rimmed baking sheet that has been lined with aluminum foil and coated with nonstick vegetable spray. Bake for 14 to 16 minutes, or until the chicken is cooked through and the juices run clear, turning halfway through the baking. Serve immediately.

Thanksgiving Tortillas

About 3 dozen slices

As a light snack or as an alternative to finger sandwiches, these tortillas taste as good as they look. And by using cranberries as a condiment, we don't add extra fat.

Four 10-inch flour tortillas
4 to 8 iceberg lettuce leaves
    (depending on size)

12 slices deli turkey
    (about 1 pound)
½ cup jellied cranberry sauce

Place 1 tortilla on a clean work surface and top with 1 or 2 lettuce leaves. Place 3 slices of turkey over the lettuce, then spoon 2 tablespoons cranberry sauce over the turkey. Roll up the tortilla and place it seam side down on a serving plate. Repeat with the remaining ingredients. Cover and refrigerate until chilled. Cut into 1-inch slices and serve.

NOTE: I like to secure each portion with a wooden toothpick before cutting.

Pinwheel Pizzas

12 mini-pinwheels

Take a "turn" with a new version of pizza. What's so different about it? It looks great and is simple to make . . . 'cause the sauce and cheese are baked right in!

1 package (10 to 11 ounces)
   refrigerated pizza crust
½ cup pizza or light spaghetti
   sauce
½ cup (2 ounces) shredded part-
   skim mozzarella cheese

½ teaspoon dried Italian
   seasoning
1 tablespoon grated Parmesan
   cheese

Preheat the oven to 425°F. Lightly flour a clean work surface. Roll the pizza dough out to a rectangle about 10" × 14", then spoon the pizza sauce evenly over the dough to the edges. Sprinkle with the mozzarella cheese and Italian seasoning. Roll up the dough jelly-roll fashion, beginning with a long end. Cut into 12 slices and place on a rimmed baking sheet that has been coated with nonstick vegetable spray. Sprinkle the slices evenly with the Parmesan cheese and bake for 12 to 14 minutes, or until the crust is golden.

NOTE: Canned refrigerated pizza crust is found in the supermarket refrigerator section along with the doughs and biscuits. For extra flavor, add a sprinkle of garlic powder, crushed red pepper, or any of your favorite spices along with the Parmesan cheese.

Buffalo Chicken Tenders

12 to 16 pieces

Buffalo-style wings sure are tasty. These days so many of us stay away from them because of their fat. Well, by using skinless chicken breast tenders that are breaded and baked, we get a way to eliminate most of the fat—but still enjoy the great taste of traditional Buffalo-style chicken wings.

½ cup all-purpose flour
½ cup hot cayenne pepper sauce
1 cup dry bread crumbs

4 boneless, skinless chicken breast halves, cut into 1-inch strips
Nonstick vegetable spray

Preheat the oven to 425°F. Place the flour, hot sauce, and bread crumbs each in its own shallow dish. Dip the chicken strips into the flour, then the hot sauce, then the bread crumbs, coating evenly with each. Place the coated strips about 1 inch apart on a baking sheet that has been coated with nonstick vegetable spray. Spray the chicken with nonstick vegetable spray and bake for about 8 minutes. Turn the chicken over and spray it with nonstick vegetable spray; cook for 2 to 3 more minutes, or until the chicken is cooked through and the breading is golden brown.

NOTE: Make sure to use hot *cayenne* pepper sauce, not simply "hot pepper sauce," . . . unless you like your chicken **really hot!**

Baked "Fried" Shrimp

36 to 40 pieces

These are like the shrimp I used to get on fisherman's platters—except those were straight from the deep fryer. With these, I've figured out a way to make them in the oven and still get that same yummy fried flavor.

1 cup self-rising flour
¼ teaspoon salt
¼ teaspoon cayenne pepper
¾ cup light beer

1 pound medium-sized shrimp, peeled, with tails left on, deveined, and rinsed

Preheat the oven to 375°F. In a medium-sized bowl, combine the flour, salt, and cayenne pepper. Pour the beer into the flour mixture and whisk until combined. Holding the shrimp by the tails, dip them into the batter, completely coating each shrimp. Place the shrimp about 4 inches apart on rimmed baking sheets that have been coated with nonstick vegetable spray. The batter will puddle around each shrimp. Bake for 12 to 14 minutes, or until the coating is golden and bread-like.

NOTE: The fish department at your supermarket will usually have cleaned and peeled shrimp available, or they'll do it for you. It sure is easier than doing it yourself!

Shortcut Clam Puffs

About 4 dozen puffs

It used to be that when we made clam puffs, we had to make the dough, then roll it. Boy, that was a lot of work! That's why I decided to top crackers with the same taste. It's much easier and just as tasty.

2 cans (6½ ounces each) chopped clams, drained
1 tablespoon chopped onion
1½ teaspoons lemon juice
2 teaspoons Worcestershire sauce

1 package (8 ounces) reduced-fat cream cheese
1 egg white
1 box (5¼ ounces) round Melba crackers

Preheat the oven to 450°F. In a medium-sized bowl, combine all the ingredients except the crackers; mix well. Place the crackers on a rimmed 10" × 15" baking sheet and top each with about a teaspoonful of the clam mixture. Bake for 7 to 9 minutes, or until lightly browned.

NOTE: I've tried this with many different crackers and decided that Melba rounds are my favorite. Use others if you'd like . . . and let me know which type you like best!

Rolled Scallops

About 30 pieces

Our supermarkets are full of foods that help us watch our fat intake. Turkey bacon is one of them, and here it is replacing the traditional pork bacon in an appetizer favorite.

1 cup barbecue sauce
¼ teaspoon hot pepper sauce
⅓ cup firmly packed light brown sugar

1 tablespoon white vinegar
6 ounces turkey bacon
1 pound sea scallops, rinsed and patted dry (see Note)

In a large bowl, combine the barbecue sauce, hot pepper sauce, brown sugar, and vinegar; stir until smooth. Cut the pieces of turkey bacon in half crosswise. Roll a piece of bacon around each scallop and secure each with a wooden toothpick. Place in the barbecue sauce mixture and toss gently to coat. Cover and chill for 20 minutes. Preheat the broiler. Place the scallop rolls on a rimmed baking sheet that has been lined with aluminum foil; discard any remaining marinade. Broil for 12 to 15 minutes, or until the scallops are cooked through.

NOTE: Be sure to use sea scallops and not bay scallops—bay scallops are too small to use in this recipe.

Tex-Mex Mini-Pizzas

16 wedges

With these individual pizzas, you get half the amount of cheese as with regular pizza, but you still get the full-bodied flavor, 'cause the salsa and beans really pack a punch!

Four 8-inch flour tortillas
Nonstick vegetable spray
1 cup salsa

1 can (16 ounces) black beans, rinsed and drained
1 cup (4 ounces) shredded Cheddar cheese

Preheat the oven to 350°F. Spray both sides of the tortillas lightly with nonstick vegetable spray and place on a rimmed baking sheet. Bake for 10 to 12 minutes, or until crisp, turning once halfway through the baking. Remove from the oven and layer evenly with the salsa, beans, and cheese. Return to the oven and bake for 5 minutes, or until the cheese is melted and the beans are hot. Cut each into 4 wedges and serve.

NOTE: If you want to cut back on fat even more, use ½ cup regular Cheddar cheese and ½ cup reduced-fat Cheddar cheese.

Mexican Chicken Bruschetta

14 to 16 slices

I love cross-cultural dishes. They're always so rich and flavorful . . . and yes, usually high in fat. Well, I've found a way to lighten this one up a bit without sacrificing flavor—simply by using a little less cheese than before.

One 1-pound loaf French or
    Italian bread, sliced in half
    lengthwise
1 cup (4 ounces) shredded
    Cheddar cheese, divided

4 cooked boneless, skinless
    chicken breast halves (1 to
    1½ pounds total), cut into
    ½-inch chunks
1 jar (16 ounces) salsa, divided
    (2 cups)

Preheat the broiler. Place the bread cut sides up on a rimmed baking sheet and broil for 3 to 5 minutes, or until light golden; leave the broiler on. Remove the bread from the broiler and top each half with ¼ cup cheese. Place the chicken chunks over the cheese. Top each bread half with 1 cup salsa. Sprinkle the remaining ½ cup cheese evenly over the salsa. Broil for 5 to 7 minutes, or until the cheese is melted and the toppings are hot. Cut into diagonal slices and serve immediately.

NOTE: When you make chicken breasts, cook extra so you've got the chicken to make this. They can be boiled, broiled, baked, grilled. And what a great way to use up French or Italian bread that's getting stale.

Jalapeño Cheese Bites

About 2 dozen pieces

Wake up lazy taste buds with these spicy bite-sized tidbits!

1 cup reduced-fat all-purpose
    baking mix
½ cup (2 ounces) shredded
    reduced-fat Monterey Jack
    cheese

2 tablespoons chopped roasted
    red peppers
1 tablespoon chopped canned
    mild jalapeño peppers
⅓ cup light beer

Preheat the oven to 450°F. In a medium-sized bowl, combine all of the ingredients except the beer; mix well. Stir in the beer and let sit for 5 minutes. Drop by teaspoonfuls onto a rimmed baking sheet that has been coated with nonstick vegetable spray. Bake for 7 to 10 minutes, or until golden. Serve hot.

NOTE: These are perfect for company, so why not make up a batch or two ahead of time, then simply rewarm them in a 200°F. oven before serving.

Black Bean Fritters

About 5 dozen fritters

So, you thought fritters had to be deep-fried? Uh-uh! You can cook 'em up just fine in a skillet with a bit of oil. And not only are we helping ourselves cut down on fat, but the black beans are full of good-for-us protein, too!

1¾ cups all-purpose flour
2 teaspoons baking powder
2 teaspoons salt
½ teaspoon black pepper
4 egg whites, beaten

1 cup salsa
2 cans (16 ounces each) black
    beans, rinsed and drained
1 tablespoon canola or vegetable
    oil, plus extra if needed

In a large bowl, combine the flour, baking powder, salt, and pepper. Add the egg whites and salsa; mix well. Stir in the black beans. Place ½ teaspoon oil in a large skillet and heat over medium-high heat. Pour 1 teaspoon of batter per fritter into the skillet, cooking several fritters at one time, but not overcrowding them. Cook for 1 minute, or until browned on the bottom, then flip the fritters and flatten them with a spatula; cook for 1 to 2 more minutes, or until browned on both sides. Repeat with the remaining batter, adding more oil as necessary.

NOTE: Serve with additional salsa and reduced-fat sour cream for dipping, if desired.

Soups

Everybody loves soup. And if you're like me, you can make a whole meal of soup alone! It's filling and it doesn't have to be loaded with fat, calories, or cholesterol. Now you'll get a chance to try some of my favorites that I have cut back a little here and there.

- Use lots of vegetables, beans, and even fruit to give your soups body. These are lighter options than heavy meats or cream when you're watching your diet. Remember, I didn't say to eliminate them, just cut back.
- When a recipe calls for heavy cream or half-and-half, try substituting reduced-fat (2%, 1%, or skim) milk or evaporated milk.
- Use reduced-sodium and reduced-fat canned soups or broths if you want the convenience of starting your own homemade soup with canned soup.
- If using homemade or canned chicken or beef broth, chill it first, then remove and discard any fat that has risen to the surface. Ice cubes will do the same thing if you place them in warm soup. Within seconds, they should rise to the surface; once the excess fat has adhered to them, use a slotted spoon to remove and discard the cubes.
- If you want to thicken your soup by letting it reduce, then cook it a bit longer than suggested—over low heat—and stir it occasionally. You can also thicken soup by slowly stirring in puréed canned beans or cooked vegetables.
- For extra flavor, use strong-flavored cheeses, like Parmesan and Romano, sparingly. You'll be surprised—a little goes a long way.

Soups

Washington Clam Chowder

6 to 8 servings

I know, I know—it's supposed to be Manhattan Clam Chowder. But there's a great little place right over the George Washington Bridge that serves a super version of this to adoring New York and New Jersey fans.

½ of a small onion, chopped
1 celery stalk, chopped
1 carrot, peeled and chopped
1 medium-sized potato, peeled and diced
3 cans (6½ ounces each) chopped clams, undrained

2 bottles (8 ounces each) clam juice
1 can (28 ounces) whole tomatoes, drained and coarsely chopped
½ teaspoon seafood seasoning

Coat a soup pot with nonstick vegetable spray. Add the onion, celery, and carrots and cook over medium heat for 3 to 5 minutes, or until the carrots are tender, stirring frequently. Add the remaining ingredients and bring to a boil, stirring occasionally. Reduce the heat to low and simmer for 8 to 10 minutes, or until the potatoes are tender.

NOTE: Make sure you have a handful of oyster crackers for topping this. There are plenty of reduced-fat brands on our market shelves.

Chunky Tomato Rice Soup

5 to 7 servings

Tomato soup is so familiar to us that we might think it's kind of boring. But what if we add some rice and chunky tomatoes? Believe me . . . instead of being bored, you're gonna be wowed!

1 can (28 ounces) whole tomatoes, coarsely chopped
2 cans (14½ ounces each) ready-to-use chicken broth
1½ cups (two 5.5-ounce cans) tomato vegetable juice

1 cup uncooked long- or whole-grain rice
1 tablespoon lemon juice
2 tablespoons dried basil
1 teaspoon garlic powder

In a large saucepan, combine all of the ingredients over medium-high heat and bring to a boil, stirring occasionally. Reduce the heat to low, cover, and simmer for 20 minutes. Remove the cover and cook for 10 more minutes. Serve hot.

NOTE: To use fresh tomatoes instead of canned, place 5 medium-sized tomatoes in a pot of boiling water for 10 seconds. Remove the tomatoes with a slotted spoon and allow to cool slightly. Peel and coarsely chop. Combine with the remaining ingredients and proceed as directed.

Vegetarian Onion Soup

4 to 6 servings

I've been getting more and more requests for vegetarian recipes, so I thought I'd try this classic with vegetable broth instead of beef. Know what? It works!

3 medium-sized onions, thinly
    sliced
3 cans (14½ ounces each) ready-
    to-use vegetable broth
1 cup water

½ cup dry red wine
½ teaspoon black pepper
½ cup grated Parmesan cheese
6 slices French bread, toasted

Coat a soup pot with nonstick vegetable spray. Add the onions and sauté over medium heat for 10 to 12 minutes, or until browned. Add the broth, water, wine, and pepper; mix well. Reduce the heat to low and simmer for 10 minutes. Add the cheese and simmer for 5 to 10 minutes, or until thoroughly blended. Pour into bowls and top each with a slice of French bread.

NOTE: If you want that traditional cheesy topping, top each slice of French bread with a slice of low-fat provolone cheese and broil or toast in a toaster oven until the cheese melts. Carefully place each one over a bowl of soup.

Hearty Minestrone Soup

8 to 10 servings

This might be called "soup," but to me it's a whole meal when served with a loaf of crusty bread.

3 cans (14½ ounces each) ready-to-use beef broth

1 can (15 to 16 ounces) red kidney beans, rinsed and drained

1 can (14 to 16 ounces) cannellini beans (white kidney beans), rinsed and drained

1 can (28 ounces) crushed tomatoes, undrained

1 package (10 ounces) frozen chopped spinach

1 package (10 ounces) frozen mixed vegetables

1 small onion, chopped

1 teaspoon garlic powder

1 teaspoon salt

½ teaspoon black pepper

1 cup uncooked elbow macaroni

In a soup pot, combine all of the ingredients except the macaroni. Bring to a boil and add the macaroni. Reduce the heat to low and simmer for 30 minutes, or until the macaroni is tender.

NOTE: If you'd like, serve this topped with a little grated Parmesan cheese. Since it's so flavorful, a little will go a long way for adding some true Italian flavor.

Creamy Mushroom Soup

4 to 5 servings

So creamy and smooth, it's hard to believe it's made without heavy cream!

1 pound fresh mushrooms, sliced
4 cups water
3 chicken bouillon cubes
½ teaspoon onion powder
½ teaspoon salt
⅛ teaspoon black pepper
1 cup low-fat milk
5 tablespoons all-purpose flour
¼ teaspoon browning and
    seasoning sauce

Coat a soup pot with nonstick vegetable spray. Add the mushrooms and sauté over medium heat for 4 to 5 minutes, or until soft. Add the water and chicken bouillon and bring to a boil; stir until the bouillon is dissolved. Reduce the heat to low and stir in the onion powder, salt, and pepper. In a measuring cup, mix the milk and flour until smooth. Gradually add to the soup, stirring constantly. Stir in the browning sauce and simmer for 5 more minutes, or until thickened. Serve immediately.

NOTE: If you want to reheat this, warm it over low heat, stirring occasionally.

Great Garlic Soup

5 to 7 servings

There must be some truth to the old story that garlic wards off evil spirits. How can I be so sure? 'Cause at my house the smell of this soup brings a happy, hungry family running to the dinner table!

7 to 8 garlic cloves, minced
3 cans (14½ ounces each) ready-
    to-use chicken broth
1½ cups water
4 slices stale or toasted bread,
    cut into ½-inch cubes

½ teaspoon black pepper
1 egg, beaten
1 scallion, chopped

Coat a medium-sized saucepan with nonstick vegetable spray. Add the garlic and lightly brown over medium heat, stirring constantly. Add the broth, water, bread, and pepper; mix well. Bring to a boil, then reduce the heat to low. Remove 2 tablespoons of the soup to a small bowl and combine with the beaten egg. Using a fork, slowly stir the egg mixture into the soup, forming egg strands. Cook for 4 to 5 minutes, until heated through. Ladle into individual bowls, top with the scallions, and serve immediately.

NOTE: Cut a garlic clove in half crosswise and rub over toasted slices of French bread for a perfect go-along.

Cream of Vegetable Soup

4 to 6 servings

When I was experimenting with this, I started with an idea for a soup like vichyssoise—a chilled potato soup. But I began adding different veggies and I turned up the temperature. Oh, yeah—I made it easy by using instant mashed potato flakes.

2 cans (14½ ounces each) ready-to-use chicken broth
1 package (16 ounces) frozen broccoli, cauliflower, and carrot combination

2½ cups low-fat milk
1½ cups instant mashed potato flakes
1 teaspoon onion powder
⅛ teaspoon black pepper

In a medium-sized saucepan, bring the broth to a boil over medium heat. Add the vegetables and return to a boil. Cover and cook for 5 minutes, or until the vegetables are tender. Stir in the remaining ingredients. Reduce the heat to low and simmer for 8 to 10 minutes, until the broth is thick and smooth, stirring occasionally.

NOTE: Any combination of frozen vegetables makes this soup truly your own—and if you have some leftover cooked or raw vegetables, sure, you can use them instead.

Turkey Kielbasa Soup

8 to 10 servings

Using turkey kielbasa gives us great sausage flavor, but with the health benefits of turkey.

6 medium-sized carrots, peeled and chopped

2 medium-sized onions, chopped

2 cans (14½ ounces each) low-sodium ready-to-use chicken broth

2 teaspoons chili powder

2 teaspoons garlic powder

1 teaspoon ground thyme

½ teaspoon black pepper

1 pound cooked turkey kielbasa, diced

1 can (28 ounces) whole tomatoes, coarsely chopped

1 can (15 to 16 ounces) red kidney beans, rinsed and drained

2 cans (15 to 16 ounces each) pinto beans, rinsed and drained

In a soup pot, combine the carrots, onions, broth, chili powder, garlic powder, thyme, and pepper over medium heat. Cook for 12 to 15 minutes, or until the onions are tender. Add the kielbasa and tomatoes. Reduce the heat to low and simmer for 45 minutes, allowing the flavors to "marry." Add the beans during the last 10 minutes of cooking.

NOTE: Sometimes I add a teaspoon of dried rosemary for a hint of extra flavor. Why don't you try it, too?

Creamy Spinach Soup

6 to 8 servings

Spinach is a great source of vitamins, and if my favorite old cartoon is any indication, this yummy soup may give your gang a super burst of energy.

8 scallions, thinly sliced
1 teaspoon minced garlic
2 cans (14½ ounces each) ready-to-use vegetable broth
2 packages (10 ounces each) frozen spinach, thawed and well drained

3 tablespoons cornstarch
3 cups low-fat milk
½ teaspoon ground nutmeg
1 teaspoon salt
½ teaspoon black pepper

Coat a large saucepan with nonstick vegetable spray. Add the scallions and garlic and sauté over medium heat for 3 to 4 minutes, or until tender. Stir in the broth and spinach. Cover and reduce the heat to low; simmer for 20 minutes. In a small bowl, combine the cornstarch and milk and stir until the cornstarch is dissolved. Pour into the soup and stir until well combined. Add the remaining ingredients and cook, stirring constantly, for 6 to 8 minutes, or until the soup has thickened. Serve immediately.

NOTE: Sometimes I add a little more garlic to really give this a nice garlic kick.

Black Bean Soup

8 to 10 servings

Quick, easy, flavorful black bean soup in a matter of minutes. . . .
And you thought making soup from scratch was going to be a challenge!

2 cans (10½ ounces each)
  condensed beef broth
3 cups water
1 medium-sized onion, chopped

4 cans (15 ounces each) black
  beans
1 jar (16 ounces) salsa (2 cups)
½ teaspoon ground cumin

In a soup pot, combine the broth, water, and onion over medium-
high heat. Cook for 5 minutes, or until the onions are tender; reduce the heat to medium-low. Meanwhile, rinse and drain 3 cans
of the beans and set aside. In a blender, purée the remaining can
of undrained beans until smooth. Add the rinsed beans and the
bean purée to the broth mixture. Stir in the salsa and cumin and
simmer for 5 minutes, until the soup is thoroughly heated, stirring
occasionally. For a thick soup, simmer it for an additional 20 to 30
minutes, stirring occasionally.

NOTE: This is even better with some additional chopped onion
and a little swirl of reduced-fat sour cream topping each serving.

Garden Pea Soup

4 to 5 servings

It sure saves time if we don't have to soak dried peas to make pea soup. And substituting imitation bacon bits for fresh bacon cuts way down on the fat.

2 packages (16 ounces each) frozen peas, thawed
2½ cups water
2 cans (10½ ounces each) condensed beef broth
3 tablespoons imitation bacon bits

½ teaspoon onion powder
¼ teaspoon browning and seasoning sauce
¼ teaspoon black pepper

In a food processor, purée the peas. Pour into a soup pot. Add the water and broth and bring to a boil over medium-high heat. Stir in the remaining ingredients and reduce the heat to medium-low. Simmer for 20 to 25 minutes, to allow the flavors to "marry."

NOTE: To make this heartier, add some chunks of leftover cooked beef or chicken breast.

Dynasty Noodle Soup

8 to 10 servings

A taste of Asia in minutes . . . without leaving your own kitchen!

4 cans (14½ ounces each) ready-to-use chicken broth

1 cup water

2 tablespoons light soy sauce

1 cup sliced fresh mushrooms

1 can (8 ounces) sliced water chestnuts, drained

1 can (8 ounces) bamboo shoots, drained

2 boneless, skinless chicken breast halves (about ½ pound total), cut into ½-inch cubes

8 ounces uncooked spaghetti, broken in half

6 scallions, sliced

In a soup pot, combine the chicken broth, water, soy sauce, mushrooms, water chestnuts, bamboo shoots, and chicken over medium-high heat and bring to a boil. Add the spaghetti and continue boiling for 8 minutes, or until the pasta is cooked. Top each serving with some of the scallions.

NOTE: Spaghetti is fine here but, if you can, try using Chinese rice noodles for an even more authentic taste. They're usually found in the ethnic section of the supermarket.

Fancy Chicken Soup

6 to 8 servings

It's no shame to start your soup with canned broth. No one will ever know.

2 medium-sized zucchini, coarsely chopped
1 medium-sized onion, coarsely chopped
1 medium-sized carrot, peeled and thinly sliced
2 cans (14½ ounces each) ready-to-use chicken broth
1½ cups coarsely chopped cooked chicken
2 cups water
½ teaspoon hot pepper sauce
1 teaspoon dried dillweed
½ teaspoon dried Italian seasoning
½ teaspoon salt

Combine all of the ingredients in a soup pot. Bring to a boil over medium-high heat and cook for 13 to 15 minutes, or until the onions are tender. Reduce the heat to low and simmer for 25 to 30 minutes.

NOTE: No chicken on hand? That's okay . . . this soup is a crowd-pleaser with or without it.

Chunky Potato Soup

4 to 6 servings

When I tell people I'm serving potato soup for dinner they ask, "Potato soup?" as if they're not sure how to respond. Well, one spoonful has them saying, "Mmm...potato soup!" again and again!

2 cups low-fat milk
1 can (10½ ounces) condensed chicken broth
1 cup water
4 medium-sized potatoes, peeled and diced

2 celery stalks, chopped
1 medium-sized onion, finely chopped
1 teaspoon salt
¼ teaspoon black pepper
1 tablespoon cornstarch

Combine all of the ingredients except the cornstarch in a soup pot. Bring to a boil over medium-high heat. Reduce the heat to low and simmer for 35 to 40 minutes, or until the potatoes are tender. Remove ¼ cup of liquid from the soup pot and combine with the cornstarch in a small bowl. Stir until the cornstarch is dissolved. Slowly pour into the soup and stir until well blended. Simmer for 10 to 15 more minutes, until the soup has thickened, stirring occasionally.

NOTE: Sometimes I like to substitute a chopped leek for the onion. That gives a classic potato and leek flavor.

Super-Easy Split Pea Soup

5 to 7 servings

For years my family begged me to re-create my grandma's split pea soup. I always avoided it because I thought it was too difficult. Well, I think this one comes really close—and it's easier! So, just add some T.L.C. and no one will know the difference.

1 bag (14 ounces) dried split peas, rinsed and cleaned according to package directions
7 cups water
2 beef bouillon cubes

1 medium-sized onion, finely chopped
1 cup grated carrots (2 to 3 carrots)
½ teaspoon salt
½ teaspoon black pepper

Combine all of the ingredients in a soup pot; mix well. Bring to a boil over medium-high heat. Reduce the heat to medium-low and simmer for 1 hour, or until the peas are soft and thoroughly cooked.

NOTE: To add a traditional smoky ham flavor, stir in 1 teaspoon of liquid smoke after the soup comes to a boil. You can find liquid smoke in the spice section of the supermarket.

Chilled Strawberry Soup

6 to 8 servings

Why not start off a summer meal with this fresh puréed fruit soup?
It's cool and refreshing, and it mixes up in a snap!

2 packages (16 ounces each)
    frozen strawberries, thawed
1 can (12 ounces) frozen apple
    juice concentrate, thawed

¼ cup water
1 tablespoon cornstarch
1 cup low-fat vanilla yogurt

In a medium-sized saucepan, combine the strawberries and apple
juice concentrate over medium heat. Bring to a boil and cook for
5 minutes. In a small bowl, combine the water and cornstarch,
stirring until smooth. Add the cornstarch mixture to the soup pot
and stir constantly for 1 minute, or until thick and clear. Allow to
cool, then pour into a blender or a food processor and purée for 5
to 10 seconds, or until the mixture is smooth and frothy. Transfer
to a large bowl, cover, and chill for 2 hours or until ready to serve.
Just before serving, stir in the yogurt.

NOTE: You can substitute 4 cups of sliced fresh strawberries for
the frozen ones if you have fresh berries on hand.

Cool Cucumber Soup

4 to 6 servings

If the expression "cool as a cucumber" never made much sense to you before, it will after you try this!

4 large cucumbers, peeled, seeded, and chopped
1 container (16 ounces) low-fat plain yogurt

1 garlic clove
¼ teaspoon dried dillweed
1 teaspoon salt

In a blender or a food processor that has been fitted with its steel cutting blade, purée all the ingredients until smooth, scraping down the sides of the blender as necessary. Transfer to a large bowl, cover, and chill for at least 2 hours, or overnight. Serve chilled.

NOTE: For an extra-sweet touch, add 1 tablespoon honey to the ingredients in the blender or food processor. And it's nice to garnish each bowl of soup with a few sprigs of fresh mint and a cucumber slice.

Chunky Veggie Gazpacho

8 to 10 servings

Imagine—something that tastes this good is so good for us!

1 can (46 ounces) tomato juice
1 can (14½ ounces) diced
    tomatoes, undrained
1 can (15 to 19 ounces) garbanzo
    beans (chick peas), rinsed
    and drained
1 package (10 ounces) frozen
    mixed vegetables, thawed
1 medium-sized onion, diced

1 medium-sized cucumber,
    peeled, seeded, and diced
1 cup water
1½ teaspoons hot pepper sauce,
    or to taste
1 tablespoon Worcestershire
    sauce
2 teaspoons dried dillweed

In a large bowl, combine all the ingredients and mix until thoroughly blended. Cover and chill for at least 2 hours, or overnight. Serve chilled.

NOTE: Depending on the brand of tomato juice you use, you may want to add ½ teaspoon of salt to bring out the other flavors. Oh— remember that with hot pepper sauce, a dash goes a long way!

Salads and Dressings

I used to hear the word *diet* and think it meant eating lots of the same boring green salads. Not anymore! Today we can really jazz up our usual greens. Also, by changing our greens often, we can keep our tossed salads interesting:

- Rotate what you use as your salad base. Instead of starting simply with iceberg lettuce, use romaine, leaf lettuce (red and green), bagged salads, spinach, and salad savoy.
- Use produce counters to their fullest. Choose add-ins of different textures, from tender mushroom slices to crunchy carrots and water chestnuts. Alternate between adding green and red cabbage, and add plain canned beans, too. (These are great ways to get lots of vitamins!)
- Add strips of grilled boneless and skinless chicken breast or fish fillets once in a while to make your salad into a smashing main dish.
- Use dressings sparingly. Pour a bit on, toss the salad lightly, and add more dressing only if the greens are really dry. Using less and really tasting your vegetables is a great start!
- Substitute fruit juice or vegetable juice for all or some of the oil in a dressing recipe.
- Try using reduced-fat sour cream or yogurt as a dressing base. Also, use reduced-fat milk in place of cream and half-and-half.
- There are lots of oils on the market; they vary by brand and type. Many oils have distinctive flavors, too, so read the product labels and try different ones in moderation, maybe lighter ones—whatever best suits your dietary needs, of course.

- Increase the ratio of vinegar to oil in your favorite vinaigrettes.
- Serve warm dressing on a cool mixed salad.
- Dressings aren't just for tossed salads. I've got fruity dressings on pages 91 to 93 that are versatile enough for topping fresh vegetables *or* fruit.

Salads and Dressings

Garden-Style Salsa Salad

4 to 6 servings

With just a few fresh vegetables, you can toss this salsa salad together in a snap for chunky homemade flavor.

4 large ripe tomatoes, finely
  chopped
1 carrot, peeled and finely
  chopped
1 medium-sized green bell pepper,
  finely chopped

1 medium-sized onion, finely
  chopped
1 tablespoon hot pepper sauce
½ teaspoon ground cumin
1 teaspoon salt

In a medium-sized bowl, combine all the ingredients; mix well. Cover and chill for at least 1 hour, or until ready to serve.

NOTE: You can keep this refrigerated for up to 1 week in an airtight container.

California Tuna Salad

4 to 6 servings

When we think of California, we think of the beautiful beaches, the excitement of Hollywood, and the glamour of Beverly Hills. When we can't visit, it's nice to be able to bring some of the sunny tastes of California to our tables.

1 large can (12 ounces) water-packed solid white tuna, drained
1 can (15 ounces) cannellini beans (white kidney beans), rinsed and drained
1 can (15 ounces) red kidney beans, rinsed and drained

½ cup hot salsa
6 scallions, chopped
1 tablespoon lemon juice
1 teaspoon minced garlic
1 teaspoon dried basil
½ teaspoon ground cumin

Flake the tuna into a large bowl; add the remaining ingredients and mix well. Cover and chill for at least 1 hour, or until ready to serve.

NOTE: To add a little extra flair, serve this on a bed of romaine or colorful salad savoy.

Strawberry Spinach Salad

6 to 8 servings

Jazz up your fresh spinach with these fresh flavors!

1 package (10 ounces) fresh
   spinach
1 pint fresh strawberries, cleaned
   and sliced lengthwise ¼ inch
   thick
½ of a small onion, finely
   chopped

3 tablespoons sugar
3 tablespoons water
2 tablespoons white vinegar
½ teaspoon dry mustard
¼ cup canola or vegetable oil

Rinse the spinach leaves and remove the stems. Dry well and tear into bite-sized pieces; place the spinach in a large salad bowl and add the strawberries. In a small bowl, combine the onion, sugar, water, vinegar, mustard, and oil. Whisk until well combined. Drizzle the dressing over the salad and toss to coat. Serve immediately.

NOTE: If you want to make this salad ahead of time, prepare the spinach, strawberries, and dressing separately and keep chilled in separate containers until ready to toss and serve.

Taco Bowl Salad

4 servings

This is so good that you'll want to eat the whole bowl . . . and you can! Yup, because your bowls are baked flour tortillas.

Four 10-inch flour tortillas, at room temperature
Nonstick vegetable spray
1 pound lean ground beef
2 tablespoons taco seasoning
⅓ cup water
½ of a medium-sized head iceberg lettuce, shredded (about 4 cups)

1 medium-sized tomato, diced
1 medium-sized green bell pepper, diced
¼ cup (1 ounce) shredded reduced-fat Cheddar cheese
2 scallions, chopped
½ cup reduced-fat sweet and spicy French dressing

Preheat the oven to 425°F. Place 4 ovenproof soup bowls on a rimmed baking sheet. Coat both sides of each tortilla with nonstick vegetable spray. Carefully mold the tortillas into the bowls. Place

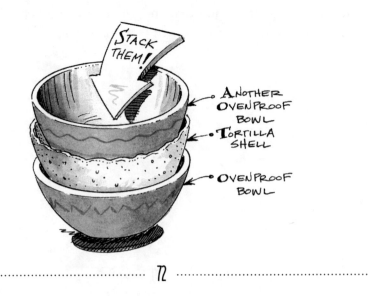

STACK THEM!

ANOTHER OVENPROOF BOWL
TORTILLA SHELL
OVENPROOF BOWL

another ovenproof soup bowl on top of each tortilla. Bake for 7 to 9 minutes, or until the tortillas hold their shape. Carefully remove the top bowls and bake the tortillas (still in the bottom bowls) for 3 to 4 more minutes, or until the tortillas are golden and crisp. (If you don't have enough bowls, bake these one or two at a time.) Remove the tortillas from the bowls and allow to cool on a wire rack. In a medium-sized skillet, brown the ground beef over medium-high heat for 10 minutes, or until no pink remains. Drain off the excess liquid. Stir in the taco seasoning and water; reduce the heat to low and simmer for 5 minutes. Place the shells on a plate and fill each ¾-full with lettuce. Add ¼ of the beef mixture, then sprinkle evenly with the tomatoes, green peppers, cheese, and scallions. Drizzle 2 tablespoons of the French dressing on top of each. Serve immediately.

Tuna Antipasto

4 servings

A typical antipasto is piled with a variety of meats and cheeses, with lots of lettuce. Not this one! It offers a feast of crunchy vegetables and tuna fish for a light, refreshing change.

1 large can (12 ounces) water-packed chunk light or solid white tuna, drained
½ of a medium-sized head iceberg lettuce, coarsely chopped (about 4 cups)
1 medium-sized tomato, cut into 1-inch chunks

1 medium-sized cucumber, peeled and cut into 1-inch chunks
1 small red onion, cut into 1-inch chunks
1 jar (16 ounces) jardinière marinated vegetables, drained
½ cup light Italian dressing

Flake the tuna into a large bowl; add the remaining ingredients and toss to mix. Serve immediately.

NOTE: Wanna make it extra-special? Use ½ cup Tomato Vinaigrette (page 97) in place of the Italian dressing.

Mandarin Spinach Salad

4 to 6 servings

Fruit juice is a great substitute for oil in salad dressing. It's low in fat and usually low in calories, yet big on flavor. Sometimes I like to add a bit of oil to give it a smooth finish.

1 can (11 ounces) mandarin
  orange segments, undrained
¼ cup white vinegar
1 tablespoon olive oil
1 tablespoon lemon juice
2 tablespoons sugar

1 package (10 ounces) fresh
  spinach
2 teaspoons dried Italian
  seasoning
4 oranges, peeled and sectioned

In a blender, combine the canned oranges (juice and all), vinegar, oil, lemon juice, and sugar. Blend until smooth. Rinse the spinach leaves and remove the stems. Dry well and place in a large salad bowl. Combine the Italian seasoning with the dressing and toss with the spinach. Top with the fresh orange sections. Serve immediately.

Lemon Couscous

8 to 12 servings

Chilled rice salads and pasta salads certainly aren't new to us—and we enjoy them. But for a change, why not use couscous as the base for a perfect go-along salad?

1 package (10 ounces) couscous
1 can (15 to 19 ounces) garbanzo
    beans (chick peas), rinsed
    and drained
¼ cup chopped fresh parsley

½ of a medium-sized red onion,
    chopped
1 medium-sized tomato, chopped
Juice of 2 lemons
¼ teaspoon black pepper

Prepare the couscous according to the package directions and allow to cool. Place in a large bowl and add the remaining ingredients; toss until well mixed. Cover and chill for at least 1 hour, or until ready to serve.

NOTE: Three to four tablespoons of bottled lemon juice will do the trick if you don't have a couple of fresh lemons on hand.

Parsley Salad

6 to 8 servings

You might know this by its traditional name, tabbouleh. It's a Middle Eastern salad packed with the fresh taste of lemon and parsley—one of my favorite herbs.

1 cup bulgur wheat
2 cups hot water
1 tablespoon olive or
    vegetable oil
⅓ cup lemon juice
1 teaspoon minced garlic
2 teaspoons dried mint
1 teaspoon salt

¼ teaspoon black pepper
1 medium-sized tomato, finely
    chopped
½ of a small cucumber, finely
    chopped
6 scallions, chopped
2 cups coarsely chopped fresh
    parsley

In a large bowl, combine the bulgur wheat and water and allow to stand for 20 to 30 minutes, or until the water is completely absorbed. Add the oil, lemon juice, garlic, mint, salt, and pepper; mix until thoroughly combined. Add the remaining ingredients and toss until blended. Cover and chill for at least 1 hour before serving.

NOTE: If chopping 2 cups of fresh parsley sounds overwhelming to you, don't let it keep you from making this. A good way to chop it without really chopping is to simply snip the parsley leaves off the stems in small pieces with kitchen shears.

Marinated Garden Salad

8 to 10 servings

I've reduced the oil, but not the taste. Oh—make sure you toss the vegetables several times so they get the full benefit of the marinade!

3 cups broccoli florets
1 small zucchini, cut into 1-inch chunks
1 small yellow squash, cut into 1-inch chunks
1 medium-sized red bell pepper, cut into 1-inch chunks
1 medium-sized red onion, cut into 1-inch chunks
½ pint cherry tomatoes, halved
¾ cup low-fat Italian dressing
¼ cup balsamic vinegar
¼ cup honey

In a large bowl, combine the broccoli, both squashes, the bell pepper, onion, and tomatoes. In a small bowl, combine the remaining ingredients; mix well. Pour over the vegetable mixture; toss until well coated. Cover and chill for at least 2 hours, or overnight, tossing occasionally.

Crazy Crab Salad

6 to 8 servings

Just glancing at these ingredients might make you think that it's a crazy combination. It is . . . it's crazy enough to be super-delicious (and really colorful, too)!

⅓ cup reduced-fat sweet and spicy French salad dressing
½ teaspoon salt
¼ teaspoon white pepper
1 can (16 ounces) sliced peaches, drained and ¼ cup juice reserved
1 can (8 ounces) sliced water chestnuts, drained

1 package (6 ounces) frozen imitation crabmeat, thawed and flaked
3 large celery stalks, thinly sliced
1 medium-sized red bell pepper, coarsely chopped

In a large bowl, combine the dressing, salt, and white pepper; mix well. Cut the peaches into 1-inch chunks and add them to the dressing, along with the reserved ¼ cup peach juice and the remaining ingredients; toss to coat. Cover and chill for at least 1 hour, or until ready to serve.

NOTE: Sliced canned pears or apricots are a nice option in place of the peaches.

Southern Slaw

8 to 10 servings

They say Southern folks make the best fried chicken and coleslaw. I hope they won't mind my lightening up their slaw a bit.

1 medium-sized head green cabbage, shredded
2 medium-sized carrots, peeled and shredded
2 tablespoons diced red onion
1 cup light mayonnaise

3 tablespoons sugar
2 tablespoons white vinegar
1 tablespoon celery seed
½ teaspoon salt
¼ teaspoon white pepper

In a large bowl, combine the cabbage, carrots, and onion; mix well. In a small bowl, combine the remaining ingredients; mix well. Pour over the cabbage mixture; toss to coat well. Cover and chill for at least 1 hour, or until ready to serve.

NOTE: Sure, you can use two 10-ounce packages of shredded cabbage and carrot mixture instead of shredding the cabbage and carrots yourself. And why not team this with Oven-Crisped Chicken (page 106) for a great Southern-style meal?

Pickled Red Beets

6 to 8 servings

When I first thought about making these, I wondered, "Who's ever gonna make fresh beets?" But I tried them anyway. And after we tasted them in my test kitchen, and I saw everybody going back for seconds and thirds, I knew these wouldn't be a problem. They're so homemade-tasting that they're worth our extra effort.

10 medium-sized fresh red beets
2 teaspoons salt, divided
½ cup sugar

1 cup water
½ cup apple cider vinegar

Cut the leafy tops off the beet stems, leaving 2 inches of stem. Place the beets in a large saucepan and add enough water to cover. Add 1 teaspoon salt and bring to a boil over medium-high heat. Reduce the heat to medium, cover, and cook for 1 hour, or until fork-tender. Drain the beets and allow to cool slightly, then slip the skins off and cut into ¼-inch slices; discard the remaining stems. Return the sliced beets to the pot and add the remaining 1 teaspoon salt, the sugar, water and cider vinegar. Bring to a boil over medium-high heat and cook for 2 to 3 minutes, or until warmed through. Transfer to a covered glass serving dish and chill overnight before serving.

NOTE: Keeping part of the stems on helps the beets keep their nice rich color. And because that color can stain your hands, you may want to wear kitchen gloves when handling the beets.

Throw-Together Carrot Salad

6 to 8 servings

If you make this according to the name, you're gonna be amazed at how easy (and fun) it is!

1 cup marshmallow creme
½ cup light mayonnaise
1 pound carrots, peeled and
　　shredded

1 can (8 ounces) pineapple
　　tidbits, well drained
½ cup raisins

In a large bowl, combine the marshmallow creme and mayonnaise until thoroughly blended. Add the remaining ingredients and toss until evenly coated. Cover and chill for at least 1 hour, or until ready to serve.

Red Potato and Bean Salad

8 to 12 servings

I've mixed up all my farm stand favorites to come up with a salad that's a real winner.

10 medium-sized red potatoes (about 3 pounds)
1 package (10 ounces) frozen cut yellow wax beans, thawed and drained
1 package (10 ounces) frozen cut green beans, thawed and drained

½ of a medium-sized red onion, coarsely chopped
¼ cup red wine vinegar
2 tablespoons olive oil
1 tablespoon sugar
1 teaspoon dried basil
1 teaspoon salt
½ teaspoon black pepper

Fill a large pot ¾-full with water and bring to a boil over medium-high heat. Add the potatoes and cook for 20 to 25 minutes, or until fork-tender. Remove from the heat and drain, reserving ¼ cup of the cooking liquid. Allow the potatoes to cool, then cut into 1-inch chunks and set aside. In a large bowl, combine the remaining ingredients, including the reserved cooking water; mix well. Add the potatoes and toss to coat. Cover and chill for at least 1 hour, or until ready to serve.

NOTE: You can use fresh beans, if you prefer. Just trim, cut in half, and add them to the potatoes for the last 10 minutes of cooking. Drain and proceed as above. And, sure, if you'd rather use all wax beans or all green beans, that'll work, too.

Curried Rice Salad

6 to 8 servings

What a cooling blend of rice and chopped vegetables! The dressing with a hint of curry makes this a super side dish.

1 cup reduced-fat Italian dressing
1 tablespoon curry powder
4 cups cold cooked long- or
　　whole-grain rice

6 scallions, chopped
4 celery stalks, finely chopped
2 medium-sized red bell peppers,
　　finely chopped

In a small bowl, combine the Italian dressing and curry powder. In a medium-sized bowl, combine the remaining ingredients. Add the dressing mixture and toss to mix. Cover and chill for at least 2 hours, or until ready to serve.

Confetti Cottage Cheese

4 servings

A colorful combination of fresh vegetables and cottage cheese sure makes a great brunch or lunch go-along—or even a refreshing low-fat snack.

1 container (16 ounces) low-fat
    cottage cheese
6 radishes, chopped
2 scallions, chopped
½ of a medium-sized cucumber,
    seeded and chopped

¼ teaspoon dried dillweed
¼ teaspoon black pepper
4 lettuce leaves

In a medium-sized bowl, combine all of the ingredients except the lettuce; mix well. Place the lettuce leaves on individual serving plates; divide the cottage cheese mixture evenly over the lettuce. Serve immediately.

NOTE: I usually use large-curd cottage cheese in this recipe because it stands up better when mixed with the veggies.

Tropical Gelatin Salad

8 to 12 servings

By removing the coconut and adding a secret ingredient, you can still have the crunch, but *not* all the fat. I know . . . that's just what you wanted!

1 package (4-serving size) lime-flavored gelatin

2 cups boiling water, divided

1 can (12 ounces) lemon-lime soda, divided

½ cup finely shredded cabbage

1 package (4-serving size) lemon-flavored gelatin

1 can (8 ounces) crushed pineapple, undrained

⅓ cup low-fat vanilla yogurt

In a medium-sized heat-proof glass bowl, combine the lime gelatin and 1 cup boiling water; stir to dissolve. Add half of the lemon-lime soda; mix well, then add the cabbage and mix again. Pour the mixture into a gelatin mold or 10-inch Bundt pan and chill for 1 hour, or until set. Combine the lemon gelatin and the remaining 1 cup boiling water in a medium-sized heat-proof glass bowl; stir to dissolve. Add the remaining ½ can soda, the pineapple (juice and all), and yogurt; whisk until smooth. Pour the mixture over the set lime gelatin mixture, cover, and chill for at least 2 hours, or until set. When ready to serve, immerse the bottom of the mold in warm water for a few seconds, then invert onto a flat serving plate larger than the mold and release the mold.

NOTE: No mold? No problem! Just make and serve it out of the glass bowl, or unmold it following the directions above.

Raspberry Fruit Cocktail

6 to 8 servings

I grew up eating canned fruit cocktail—we all loved it back then. But now that there's so much more fresh fruit available for salads like this one, I don't know if I'll ever go back to canned!

1 cup water
½ cup sugar
1 teaspoon cornstarch
½ pint fresh raspberries, gently washed and patted dry

2 large grapefruit, peeled and sectioned
3 large navel oranges, peeled and sectioned
2 large pears, cored and sliced

In a medium-sized saucepan, combine the water, sugar, and cornstarch over medium-high heat; bring to a boil, stirring until the sugar and cornstarch are dissolved. Add the raspberries and cook for 3 to 5 minutes, or until the mixture is slightly thickened; remove from the heat and allow to cool. In a large bowl, combine the grapefruit, oranges, and pears. Pour the cooled raspberry mixture over the fruit and toss to coat. Cover and chill for at least 1 hour, or until ready to serve.

NOTE: If you want to use frozen raspberries, increase the cornstarch to 1 tablespoon, use 1½ cups frozen raspberries (about ½ of a 12-ounce package), and cook the raspberries for 5 to 7 minutes; then proceed as above.

Light 'n' Easy Ambrosia

6 to 8 servings

By reducing the amount of coconut and using low-fat yogurt instead of whipped cream, I've come up with a way to reduce the fat without sacrificing the flavor of everybody's favorite ambrosia.

1 can (20 ounces) pineapple
  chunks, drained
1 jar (10 ounces) maraschino
  cherries, drained and halved

2 cups miniature marshmallows
1 cup low-fat vanilla yogurt
½ cup flaked coconut

In a large bowl, combine all of the ingredients and toss until evenly coated with the yogurt. Cover and chill for at least 1 hour, or until ready to serve.

NOTE: This makes a super side dish or a nice light dessert.

Waldorf Salad

4 to 6 servings

Here's a fruity salad with loads of richness tossed in. And since we replaced half of the usual amount of mayonnaise with marshmallow creme, we can enjoy this without worrying so much about the fat numbers!

¼ cup orange juice
½ cup light mayonnaise
½ cup marshmallow creme
¼ teaspoon salt
2 celery stalks, chopped
1 cup red seedless grapes, cut
    in half

4 Red Delicious apples, cored and
    cut into 1-inch chunks
2 tablespoons chopped walnuts
    (see Note)

In a large bowl, whisk together the orange juice, mayonnaise, marshmallow creme, and salt until well combined. Add the remaining ingredients except the walnuts and toss to coat. Cover and chill for at least 1 hour, or until ready to serve. Just before serving, sprinkle the top with the chopped walnuts.

NOTE: When you're trying to cut down on fat, most people will tell you to stay away from nuts. But walnuts are known to be high in polyunsaturated fats—the "good" fats. And some studies have even shown that walnuts help reduce the risk of heart disease. Check with your doctor and, if it's okay, then go ahead and use them to top your Waldorf Salad.

Cranberry Holiday Mold

10 to 12 servings

Cranberries used to make their appearance only on holiday dinner tables. But with today's year-round availability in so many forms, I like to make any day into a holiday!

2 packages (4-serving size) cranberry- or strawberry-flavored gelatin
1 cup boiling water
1 can (16 ounces) whole-berry cranberry sauce

1½ cups cold ginger ale
1 can (11 ounces) mandarin orange segments, drained

In a large heat-proof bowl, combine the gelatin and boiling water; stir to dissolve. Add the cranberry sauce; mix well. Stir in the ginger ale, then pour into a gelatin mold or 10-inch Bundt pan. Place the orange segments over the top and chill for at least 4 hours, or until firm. When ready to serve, immerse the bottom of the mold in warm water for a few seconds, then invert onto a flat serving plate larger than the mold and release the mold.

NOTE: Diet ginger ale will work just as well as regular, while reducing the sugar content of this treat.

Spicy Apricot Fruit Dressing

About 1 1/2 cups

Over fresh fruit? Sure! Over mixed greens? Definitely! Over fruit pies and ice cream? Yes, yes, yes!

½ cup apricot nectar
½ cup reduced-fat sour cream
½ cup low-fat vanilla yogurt

3 tablespoons sugar
½ teaspoon ground cinnamon
⅛ teaspoon salt

In a medium-sized bowl, combine all the ingredients and whisk until smooth and creamy. Store in the refrigerator in an airtight container until ready to use.

NOTE: Serve this over fresh-cut fruit such as cantaloupe, honeydew, red and green grapes, fresh berries, or your other fruit and veggie favorites.

Honey-Lime Fruit Dressing

About 1½ cups

Fresh fruit is a great snack when we're watching our calories, fat, and refined sugar. But I know that it's easy to get bored with it as is. So end the ho-hum by dressing your fresh-cut fruits with this light dressing.

1 cup low-fat vanilla yogurt
½ cup honey
Juice of 1 lime

¼ teaspoon grated lime zest
¼ teaspoon salt

In a medium-sized bowl, combine all the ingredients and whisk until smooth and creamy. Store in the refrigerator in an airtight container until ready to use.

NOTE: Make a batch to keep on hand. That way, when you're ready to nibble on some fruit, you're all set.

Orange-Honey Dressing

About 1 cup

Russian dressing, Italian dressing, French dressing—we're used to those, and we can make 'em or buy 'em. But for those times when we're looking for a way to really stimulate our taste buds, this home-made dressing will do the trick.

½ cup orange juice

⅓ cup red wine vinegar

2 tablespoons honey

1 tablespoon olive oil

1 teaspoon salt

½ teaspoon black pepper

Combine all the ingredients in a medium-sized bowl and whisk until thoroughly mixed. Store in the refrigerator in an airtight container until ready to use.

NOTE: Serve over fresh mixed greens and top with fresh orange sections, if you've got 'em.

Creamy Balsamic Dressing

About 2 cups

I like to toss this with lots of crisp greens. That way the salad is nicely coated, without drowning it in dressing.

1 cup low-fat plain yogurt
¼ cup light mayonnaise
3 tablespoons Dijon-style mustard

2 tablespoons lemon juice
⅓ cup balsamic vinegar
1 tablespoon dried parsley flakes

In a small bowl, combine all the ingredients and blend with a spoon or whisk until smooth and creamy. Store in the refrigerator in an airtight container until ready to use.

NOTE: After you've tried mixing this with your favorite fresh greens, why not try serving it the next time over steamed fresh vegetables?

Honey-Mustard Dressing

About 1 ¼ cups

By using a light mayonnaise here, you're cutting down on the fat, but *not* on that great honey-mustard flavor.

1 cup light mayonnaise
¼ cup honey
1 tablespoon white vinegar
2 tablespoons prepared yellow
    mustard

2 tablespoons dried parsley flakes
1 teaspoon onion powder

In a medium-sized bowl, combine all the ingredients and whisk until smooth and creamy. Store in the refrigerator in an airtight container until ready to use.

NOTE: Whether I use this as an accompaniment to chicken or on a tossed salad, it's one of my favorite dressings.

Light Caesar Dressing

About 2 cups

If you love Caesar salad, like me, then you'll be pleasantly surprised by how flavorful this light version is.

1 cup light mayonnaise
¾ cup low-fat milk
1 tablespoon Dijon-style mustard
2 tablespoons lemon juice

½ cup grated Parmesan cheese
½ teaspoon garlic powder
½ teaspoon salt
½ teaspoon black pepper

In a medium-sized bowl, combine all the ingredients and whisk until smooth and creamy. Store in the refrigerator in an airtight container until ready to toss with salad greens.

NOTE: You can make a quick and light Caesar salad by tossing this dressing with torn romaine lettuce and croutons. (And you can make some quick croutons by cutting day-old bread into 1-inch cubes, tossing with some garlic powder, salt, and black pepper, and toasting in a 300°F. oven until brown.)

Tomato Vinaigrette

About 2 cups

By cutting back on the oil and adding a few extra spices, I've whipped up a vinaigrette that you can enjoy using again and again . . . without any guilt!

1 cup water
¾ cup red wine vinegar
3 tablespoons olive oil
2 tablespoons tomato paste
1 tablespoon sugar

1 tablespoon dried Italian
    seasoning
¼ teaspoon garlic powder
½ teaspoon salt

Combine all the ingredients in a blender and blend on high speed for 5 to 10 seconds, or until well blended. Store in the refrigerator in an airtight container until ready to use.

NOTE: You can use this as a dressing for tossed salads or pasta salads and also as a vegetable marinade.

Farmer's Dressing

About 2 ¼ cups

I included this recipe in an early book and have consistently received raves on it. So I figured I should lighten up that version and share it with you here.

1 medium-sized cucumber, cut
    into 1-inch chunks
1 cup reduced-fat sour cream

1 cup light mayonnaise
½ teaspoon garlic powder
¼ teaspoon black pepper

In a blender or in a food processor that has been fitted with its steel cutting blade, combine all the ingredients and process until smooth and creamy. Store in the refrigerator in an airtight container until ready to use.

NOTE: For a change of pace, try serving this creamy, delightful dressing over your favorite mixed greens or simply over fresh-cut cucumbers.

POULTRY

Poultry

If you think eating lighter is "for the birds," you're right! What I mean is, when you're watching yourself, you can enjoy a good selection of poultry dishes if you follow a few basic guidelines:

- Get naked—no, not the cook, the bird! Remove the skin from all the parts before cooking; that cuts the fat content of the chicken by about 50 percent. Some people like to cook chicken with the skin on, then remove it before serving. Sure, it tastes good that way, but it doesn't reduce the fat by as much as when you remove the skin before cooking.
- Keep in mind that white-meat poultry (breast meat) is leaner than dark meat (thighs and legs).
- Rack 'em up! Whenever possible, place your whole bird on a roasting rack or vertical roaster to allow the fat to drip off it and into the roasting pan.
- Remember that turkey is not just for holidays! It's a great source of protein, it's low in fat and cholesterol, it's available in many forms (whole, parts, ground, even sausage!). Oh, of course ground turkey *breast* is the leanest type of ground turkey.
- Skim fat from pan drippings before using them for sauces or gravies.
- Avoid self-basting or flavor-enriched whole turkeys. When you make your own basting mixtures, you can control what you roast with. Use one or more of the following: fruit juices, honey, defatted broth, wine, and seasonings.

Poultry

Sweet-and-Sour Chicken

4 servings

One of my kitchen assistants loves sweet-and-sour chicken so much that that's what she orders every time she goes out for Chinese food. So when it came time to create a light version, I knew just who could help me capture the authentic flavor. Thanks, Patty!

2 teaspoons canola or vegetable oil, divided

4 boneless, skinless chicken breast halves (1 to 1¼ pounds total)

3 medium-sized carrots, peeled and sliced

1 large green bell pepper, cut into 1-inch chunks

1 can (20 ounces) pineapple chunks, drained and juice reserved

¼ cup firmly packed light brown sugar

3 tablespoons white vinegar

2 tablespoons soy sauce

2 tablespoons water

1 tablespoon cornstarch

In a large skillet, heat 1 teaspoon oil over medium-high heat. Add the chicken and brown for 3 to 4 minutes on each side. Remove the chicken from the skillet; set aside. Add the remaining 1 teaspoon oil to the skillet and heat over medium-high heat. Add the carrots and green pepper and sauté for 4 to 5 minutes, until tender. Reduce the heat to medium and add the reserved pineapple juice, the brown sugar, vinegar, and soy sauce; cook until hot. In a small bowl, combine the water and cornstarch and whisk until smooth. Slowly add to the pineapple juice mixture and bring to a boil, stirring occasionally until thickened. Reduce the heat to low and add the pineapple chunks and chicken breasts; simmer for 10 minutes, or until the chicken is cooked through and no pink remains.

Oven-Crisped Chicken

4 to 6 servings

Crunch, crunch, crunch. That's the only sound you'll hear after you bring a platter of this to the table. Well, after a while you'll certainly hear everyone asking for more!

1 chicken (2½ to 3 pounds), cut into 8 pieces and skin removed
2 teaspoons salt
1 teaspoon black pepper
⅔ cup all-purpose flour
½ cup egg substitute
¼ cup low-fat milk
6 cups oven-toasted rice cereal, coarsely crushed
1 teaspoon garlic powder

Preheat the oven to 350°F. Sprinkle the chicken with the salt and pepper. Place the flour in a shallow dish. In a small bowl, combine the egg substitute and milk; whisk until well combined. In a large bowl, combine the cereal crumbs and garlic powder; toss to mix well. Coat a large roasting rack with nonstick vegetable spray and place in a large roasting pan. Dip the chicken in the flour mixture, then the egg mixture, then the cereal mixture, completely coating it each time. Place the coated chicken on the rack in the roasting pan. Bake for 50 to 55 minutes, or until no pink remains and the juices run clear.

Fast Chicken Fajitas

10 fajitas

Sure, you can go to a trendy restaurant to order these, but usually when you get past the steam and the sizzle, you're left with a small portion of chicken and a high price tag! So, why not bring the sizzle to your own kitchen table—with a lower calorie count *and* a lower price tag!

1 tablespoon vegetable oil
2 large onions, cut into 8 wedges each
1 large green bell pepper, cut into ½-inch strips
1 large red bell pepper, cut into ½-inch strips
4 boneless, skinless chicken breast halves (1 to 1¼ pounds total), cut into ½-inch strips

2 tablespoons dry fajita seasoning
Ten 8-inch flour tortillas
1 cup salsa
½ of a medium-sized head iceberg lettuce, shredded (about 4 cups)

In a large skillet, heat the oil over medium-high heat. Add the onions and peppers and sauté for 3 to 5 minutes, or until the onions are tender, stirring occasionally. In a small bowl, combine the chicken and the fajita seasoning and toss until the chicken is thoroughly coated. Add to the skillet and cook for 5 to 6 minutes, or until no pink remains in the chicken and the onions are browned, stirring frequently. Distribute the chicken mixture evenly over the tortillas. Top with the salsa and lettuce, then roll up the tortillas and serve immediately.

Always-Apricot Chicken

3 to 4 servings

Fresh apricots have a really short season. But by using canned apricots and bottled apricot preserves, we can extend their season to last us the whole year!

1 chicken (2½ to 3 pounds), cut into 8 pieces and skin removed
2 cans (5½ ounces each) apricot nectar
1 jar (18 ounces) apricot preserves

1 teaspoon ground allspice
⅛ teaspoon ground ginger
½ teaspoon salt
¼ teaspoon black pepper

Place the chicken in a 9" × 13" glass baking dish that has been coated with nonstick vegetable spray. In a medium-sized bowl, combine the remaining ingredients; mix well. Pour over the chicken and cover tightly with aluminum foil. Refrigerate overnight, turning the chicken occasionally. Preheat the oven to 350°F. Bake the chicken, covered, for 30 minutes. Remove the foil and bake for 25 to 30 more minutes, or until no pink remains and the juices run clear.

NOTE: I recommend buying the small individual-serving size cans of apricot nectar. That way you can always keep some on hand in the cupboard for when you want to whip this up for dinner.

American Pie Chicken

4 servings

Apple pie topped with a wedge of Cheddar cheese . . . how American and how delicious! That's why I decided to top chicken breasts with those same tastes to get a taste worthy of a salute.

4 boneless, skinless chicken
    breast halves (1 to 1¼
    pounds total)
½ teaspoon salt

⅛ teaspoon black pepper
½ cup apple butter
¼ cup (1 ounce) shredded
    Cheddar cheese

Preheat the oven to 350°F. Place the chicken in a 7" × 11" glass baking dish that has been coated with nonstick vegetable spray. Sprinkle with the salt and pepper, then spread the apple butter evenly over the chicken. Cover with aluminum foil and bake for 25 to 30 minutes, or until the juices run clear. Remove from the oven, uncover, and sprinkle the cheese evenly over the top of the chicken. Return to the oven and bake, uncovered, for 4 to 6 minutes, or until the cheese is melted.

NOTE: Apple butter can be found in the jelly and jam section of your supermarket. And, contrary to its name, it does *not* contain butter.

Hot 'n' Spicy Orange Chicken

4 to 6 servings

You thought cooking lighter was boring . . . ? No way!

4 teaspoons soy sauce
¼ teaspoon salt
¼ teaspoon black pepper
1 whole chicken (2½ to 3
    pounds), skin removed

2 oranges, quartered
½ cup orange marmalade
1 teaspoon hot pepper sauce

Preheat the oven to 350°F. Line a 9" × 13" baking pan with aluminum foil and coat with nonstick vegetable spray. In a small bowl, combine the soy sauce, salt, and pepper. Rub the inside and outside of the chicken with the mixture. Stuff the chicken with the orange quarters. Place the chicken breast side up in the baking pan. Coat the outside of the chicken with the orange marmalade and drizzle with the hot pepper sauce. Bake for 1¼ to 1½ hours, or until no pink remains and the juices run clear. Discard the oranges, cut the chicken into serving-sized pieces, and then drizzle with the pan juices.

Herb-Crusted Chicken

4 to 6 servings

Mmm . . . crispy on the outside, juicy on the inside. And since we remove the skin before baking, we cut out about half the fat—but still get plenty of flavor from all the herbs.

2 tablespoons dried basil
2 tablespoons dried oregano
2 tablespoons dried rosemary
2 tablespoons dried thyme
1 teaspoon salt

¼ cup dry bread crumbs
1 chicken (2½ to 3 pounds), cut
    into 8 pieces and skin
    removed
Nonstick vegetable spray

Preheat the oven to 425°F. In a medium-sized bowl, combine all the ingredients except the chicken and the spray; mix well. Coat a nonstick rimmed baking sheet with nonstick vegetable spray. Completely coat the chicken pieces with the crumb mixture and place 1 inch apart on the baking sheet. Spray the chicken with nonstick vegetable spray and bake for 40 to 45 minutes, or until no pink remains and the juices run clear.

Curried Chicken

4 servings

Just five easy ingredients to an Indian-style meal that's worth its weight in gold. Got some "karats" to serve with it? (Really, it's nice served with steamed carrots.)

1½ teaspoons curry powder
1 teaspoon onion powder
1 teaspoon ground cumin
½ teaspoon salt

4 boneless, skinless chicken
breast halves (1 to 1¼
pounds total)

Preheat the oven to 350°F. In a small bowl, combine all the ingredients except the chicken; mix well. Rub the entire chicken with the seasoning mixture. Place the chicken on a 10" × 15" rimmed baking sheet that has been coated with nonstick vegetable spray. Bake for 15 to 20 minutes, or until no pink remains and the juices run clear.

French Diner Chicken

6 servings

Living in South Florida, I take every chance I get to eat in a little French diner near South Beach (a really "happening" area). One of my favorite meals there is a chicken dish prepared like this.

¼ cup all-purpose flour
6 boneless, skinless chicken
    breast halves (1½ to 2
    pounds total)
1 tablespoon olive oil
3 garlic cloves, crushed
2 medium-sized onions, cut in
    half and sliced

2 medium-sized red bell peppers,
    cut into ¼-inch strips
½ cup dry white wine
1 chicken bouillon cube
½ teaspoon salt
½ teaspoon black pepper

Preheat the oven to 350°F. Place the flour in a shallow dish. Coat the chicken pieces with the flour. Heat the olive oil in a large nonstick skillet over medium-high heat. Add the garlic and chicken and cook the chicken for 3 to 4 minutes on each side, or until golden brown. Remove the chicken from the skillet and place in a 9" × 13" baking dish that has been coated with nonstick vegetable spray. Add the onions and bell peppers to the skillet and cook, stirring occasionally, for 5 to 8 minutes, until the peppers are crisp-tender. Spoon the vegetables evenly over the chicken breasts. Add the wine, bouillon, salt, and pepper to the skillet and stir until the bouillon is dissolved. Pour the wine mixture over the chicken; cover with aluminum foil and bake for 20 to 25 minutes, or until the chicken is cooked through and no pink remains.

"Let-Us" Roast Chicken

4 to 6 servings

At first glance you're going to think I've made a mistake in these directions—cover a chicken with lettuce leaves?! Yup! The lettuce helps hold in the moisture and keeps the spices from burning. It actually acts like the skin when the chicken roasts.

1 whole chicken (2½ to 3 pounds), skin removed
½ teaspoon paprika
½ teaspoon garlic powder
½ teaspoon onion powder

½ teaspoon salt
⅛ teaspoon black pepper
4 to 5 large iceberg lettuce leaves, washed and patted dry

Preheat the oven to 350°F. Place the chicken breast side up in a 9" × 13" baking dish. In a small bowl, combine the remaining ingredients except the lettuce; mix well. Rub the chicken evenly with the spice mixture, then lay the lettuce leaves over the top, curving them around and completely covering the chicken. Bake for 65 to 70 minutes, or until the juices run clear and no pink remains. Discard the lettuce leaves before serving.

THE CHICKEN!

WRAPPED!

No-Fry Honey Chicken

4 to 6 servings

No deep fryer needed here! As a matter of fact, there isn't even any oil needed, since it's not fried. But the coating is extra-crispy just the same.

1 cup honey
2 cups cornflake crumbs

1 chicken (2½ to 3 pounds), cut into 8 pieces and skin removed

Preheat the oven to 350°F. Place the honey in a shallow bowl. Place the cornflake crumbs in another shallow bowl. Dip the chicken into the honey, then into the cornflake crumbs, completely coating the chicken each time. Place the chicken in a 9" × 13" glass baking dish that has been coated with nonstick vegetable spray. Bake for 55 to 60 minutes, or until golden brown and the juices run clear.

NOTE: Check out the honey section of your supermarket. Each different kind of honey will give this dish a unique taste. My favorite is the most common type—clover honey.

Chicken in a Pot

4 to 6 servings

An all-in-one meal that not only tastes good but is also good for you. Well, that's what my grandmother used to tell me.

1 whole chicken (2½ to 3 pounds), cut into 8 pieces and skin removed
6 medium-sized carrots, peeled and cut into 1-inch pieces
4 large celery stalks, cut into 1-inch pieces
2 medium-sized onions, cut into 8 wedges each
5 cups water
1 chicken bouillon cube
2 teaspoons salt
½ teaspoon black pepper

In a soup pot, combine all of the ingredients and bring to a boil over high heat. Reduce the heat to medium-low, cover, and cook for 1 hour, or until the chicken is "fall-apart" tender.

NOTE: You can add additional vegetables, such as potatoes, zucchini, or even garbanzo beans (chick peas), for fresh garden flavor.

Jammin' Chicken

4 servings

When people get together to play really good, upbeat music, some people say they're "jammin'." And I say that when chicken is this good it deserves the same description. Oh, and the raspberry jam is what gives it the really "jammin'" taste!

4 chicken leg-thigh quarters
   (3½ to 4 pounds total),
   skin removed
½ teaspoon salt
½ teaspoon black pepper

½ cup seedless red raspberry jam
2 tablespoons balsamic vinegar
1 tablespoon light soy sauce
⅛ teaspoon crushed red pepper

Preheat the oven to 375°F. Place the chicken in a 9" × 13" glass baking dish that has been coated with nonstick vegetable spray; sprinkle with the salt and black pepper. In a small saucepan, combine the remaining ingredients over low heat for about 1 minute, or until the jam melts and the sauce is smooth and bubbly. Spoon half of the raspberry mixture over the chicken. Cover with aluminum foil and bake for 50 to 55 minutes, or until no pink remains and the juices run clear. Remove from the oven. Spoon the remaining sauce over the chicken, and bake for 5 minutes, uncovered, or until the sauce glazes the chicken.

NOTE: Apple cider vinegar will do if you don't have any balsamic vinegar.

Chicken in Lime Sauce

4 servings

Need a tropical fix? Here's where you get on!

4 boneless, skinless chicken
    breast halves (1 to 1¼
    pounds total)
2 teaspoons lime juice
Peel from ½ of a medium-sized
    lime, cut into ⅛-inch strips

¾ cup apple juice
1 chicken bouillon cube
2 teaspoons cornstarch

Coat a medium-sized skillet with nonstick vegetable spray. Add the chicken and cook over medium heat for 6 to 8 minutes, or until browned, turning once. Meanwhile, in a small saucepan, combine the remaining ingredients over medium heat and simmer for 3 to 4 minutes, or until the bouillon dissolves and the mixture thickens. Pour the sauce over the chicken, cover, and cook for 10 to 12 minutes, or until the juices run clear and no pink remains.

NOTE: For an extra-tropical flavor, try using Key limes when they're available. Key limes are native to the Florida Keys and are smaller, lighter in color, and more intense in flavor than regular limes.

Lemon-Roasted Chicken

4 to 6 servings

By removing the skin and covering the chicken with thin lemon slices, you reduce the fat but keep the moisture in. And oh, that lemon flavor!

1 chicken (2½ to 3 pounds), cut into 8 pieces and skin removed
2 teaspoons dried oregano
¼ teaspoon salt
¼ teaspoon black pepper
3 lemons, thinly sliced
1 medium-sized onion, thinly sliced

Preheat the oven to 400°F. Place the chicken pieces in a 9" × 13" glass baking dish that has been coated with nonstick vegetable spray. Sprinkle the chicken with the oregano, salt, and pepper. Place the lemon slices evenly over the chicken. Place the onion slices over the lemon slices, then tightly cover the dish with aluminum foil. Bake for 45 minutes, then uncover and bake for 10 to 15 more minutes, or until the juices run clear and no pink remains.

NOTE: For mixed citrus flavor, I've made this with 1 lemon, 1 lime, and 1 orange instead of 3 lemons. Try it!

Oven-Barbecued Chicken

4 to 6 servings

This is an all-time favorite that's made better by using skinless chicken. That means we can savor every drop of barbecue flavor—without extra fat.

1 chicken (2½ to 3 pounds), cut into 8 pieces and skin removed
1 tablespoon all-purpose flour
1 cup ketchup
1 small onion, finely chopped
¼ cup firmly packed light brown sugar

2 tablespoons white vinegar
2 tablespoons Worcestershire sauce
2 tablespoons prepared yellow mustard

Preheat the oven to 400°F. Place the chicken pieces in a 9" × 13" glass baking dish that has been coated with nonstick vegetable spray. Sprinkle the chicken with the flour. In a small bowl, combine the remaining ingredients; mix well. Pour evenly over the chicken and cover tightly with aluminum foil. Bake for 30 minutes, then uncover and bake for 30 to 35 more minutes, or until the juices run clear and no pink remains.

NOTE: If you want, you can bake these for 30 minutes, then finish them off on the grill until no pink remains.

South Pacific Chicken

4 to 6 servings

C'mon, be adventurous with some "direct from the tropics" flavor. . . .

1 chicken (2½ to 3 pounds), cut into 8 pieces and skin removed
1 can (8 ounces) crushed pineapple, undrained
¼ cup drained maraschino cherries

⅓ cup sugar
2 tablespoons light soy sauce
¼ teaspoon garlic salt
⅛ teaspoon ground ginger
1 orange, peeled and sliced ¼ inch thick
1 tablespoon cornstarch

Preheat the oven to 350°F. Place the chicken pieces in a 9" × 13" glass baking dish that has been coated with nonstick vegetable spray. In a medium-sized bowl, combine the remaining ingredients except the orange slices and cornstarch; mix well. Pour over the chicken, then place the orange slices evenly over the top. Cover with aluminum foil and bake for 50 minutes. Remove the foil and bake for 10 to 15 more minutes, or until the juices run clear and no pink remains. Place the chicken on a serving platter; cover to keep warm. Pour the pan drippings into a medium-sized saucepan. In a small bowl, combine 2 tablespoons of the drippings with the cornstarch; stir until smooth. Stir the cornstarch mixture into the drippings and cook over medium-high heat for 2 to 3 minutes, or until clear and thick. Pour the sauce over the chicken.

"Naked" Chicken

4 servings

The good thing about this "naked" chicken is that you get to "dress it up."

2 teaspoons paprika
1 teaspoon garlic powder
1 teaspoon onion powder
1 teaspoon salt
¼ teaspoon black pepper

⅛ teaspoon cayenne pepper
1 chicken (2½ to 3 pounds), cut
    into quarters and skin
    removed

Preheat the oven to 450°F. In a small bowl, combine all the ingredients except the chicken; mix well. Rub the spice mixture over the chicken, coating evenly. Individually wrap each quarter in aluminum foil, sealing tightly. Place the foil packets on a large rimmed baking sheet and bake for 40 to 45 minutes, or until the juices run clear and no pink remains. Use 2 forks to pry the packets open. **Steam will be released when the foil packets are opened, so be careful!**

NOTE: You can also make "Naked" Chicken on the grill—just put the foil packets on the grill rack and cook for 35 to 40 minutes, or until the juices run clear and no pink remains, turning the packets occasionally.

Tandoori Chicken

4 to 6 servings

Indian foods are surprisingly low in fat, yet they're packed with flavor. That's because they're so heavily seasoned. Give this one a try!

1½ cups low-fat plain yogurt
2 tablespoons hot pepper sauce
8 to 10 drops red food color
   (optional)
1 teaspoon ground ginger
1 teaspoon ground cumin
1 teaspoon crushed red pepper
1 teaspoon paprika

½ teaspoon garlic powder
½ teaspoon ground coriander
⅛ teaspoon ground cloves
1 teaspoon salt
⅛ teaspoon black pepper
1 chicken (2½ to 3 pounds), cut
   into 8 pieces and skin
   removed

Preheat the oven to 450°F. Place all the ingredients except the chicken in a medium-sized bowl; mix well. Coat the chicken evenly with the mixture and place on a 10" × 15" rimmed baking sheet that has been lined with aluminum foil and coated with nonstick vegetable spray. Bake for 45 to 50 minutes, or until the juices run clear and no pink remains.

Brunswick Stew

4 to 6 servings

A nice change from traditional beef stew, this hearty chicken and vegetable dish will satisfy the hungriest of appetites.

2 large onions, cut into ¼-inch slices

1 chicken (2½ to 3 pounds), cut into 8 pieces and skin removed

1 can (28 ounces) crushed tomatoes, undrained

½ cup water

1 package (16 ounces) frozen vegetable gumbo mix, thawed (see Note)

1 package (10 ounces) frozen lima beans, thawed

½ cup barbecue sauce

1 teaspoon garlic powder

1 teaspoon salt

¾ teaspoon black pepper

Coat a soup pot with nonstick vegetable spray. Add the onions and cook over medium heat for 3 to 4 minutes, until lightly browned. Add the chicken and cook for about 5 minutes, turning until lightly browned. Add the remaining ingredients and bring to a boil. Reduce the heat to low and cover; simmer for 2 hours, or until the chicken falls off the bones.

NOTE: Frozen vegetable gumbo mix usually includes okra, corn, onion, celery, and bell peppers. If you want, you can substitute your favorite frozen vegetable combination.

Hoppin' John

6 to 8 servings

I got a Hoppin' John recipe from a viewer who swears that you have to use leftover holiday ham in it. Since I tried this when I didn't have any leftovers, I replaced the ham with turkey sausage and ended up with quite a satisfying dish. Try it either way.

1 pound turkey sausage, casings removed

5 medium-sized carrots, peeled and chopped

1 medium-sized onion, chopped

1 medium-sized red bell pepper, chopped

2 garlic cloves, chopped

3 cans (14½ ounces each) ready-to-use chicken broth

2 cans (15½ ounces each) black-eyed peas, rinsed and drained

¾ teaspoon dried rosemary

½ teaspoon ground thyme

¼ teaspoon cayenne pepper

3 cups instant white or brown rice

Coat a large soup pot with nonstick vegetable spray. Add the sausage, carrots, onion, bell pepper, and garlic and cook over medium-high heat for 7 to 8 minutes, or until the sausage is no longer pink. Remove from the heat and drain off the excess liquid. Add the broth, black-eyed peas, rosemary, thyme, and cayenne pepper. Bring to a boil, cover, and reduce the heat to low; simmer for 5 to 6 minutes, or until the carrots are tender. Add the rice, increase the heat to medium-high, and return the mixture to a boil. Cover and remove from the heat; let stand for 5 minutes before serving.

Turkey Cacciatore

4 to 6 servings

I've got a load of fresh vegetables in here with turkey breast—no dark-meat turkey. That way you can still enjoy the classic old-world tastes, but with less fat.

1 tablespoon olive oil
2 medium-sized bell peppers (any color), thinly sliced
1 large onion, halved and cut into ¼-inch slices
5 ounces fresh mushrooms, sliced (about 2 cups)

1½ to 2 pounds uncooked boneless, skinless turkey breast, cut into 1-inch chunks
1 jar (28 ounces) light spaghetti sauce
½ cup water
¼ teaspoon black pepper

In a large saucepan, heat the oil over medium-high heat. Add the bell peppers, onion, and mushrooms and sauté for 4 to 5 minutes, or until tender. Push the vegetables to one side of the pan and add the turkey. Cook for about 5 minutes, or until the outside of the turkey is no longer pink. Stir in the spaghetti sauce, water, and black pepper. Reduce the heat to medium-low and continue cooking for 25 to 30 minutes, or until the turkey is tender and cooked through, stirring occasionally.

NOTE: You can serve this over warm cooked noodles or pasta for a complete meal.

Barbecued Turkey Loaf

4 to 6 servings

Okay, after sharing so many recipes with you I guess I can tell you the secret ingredient that makes this recipe so light. Promise you won't tell . . . it's the rolled oats. Shh. . . .

6 tablespoons barbecue sauce, divided

2 tablespoons water

⅔ cup quick-cooking or old-fashioned rolled oats

2 egg whites, lightly beaten

2 teaspoons chili powder

2 teaspoons Worcestershire sauce

½ teaspoon salt

1 to 1¼ pounds ground turkey breast

⅔ cup finely chopped onion

⅓ cup chopped red or green bell pepper

Preheat the oven to 375°F. In a large bowl, combine 3 tablespoons barbecue sauce and the water. Add the oats, egg whites, chili powder, Worcestershire sauce, and salt; mix well. Add the remaining ingredients except the reserved barbecue sauce; mix well. Pat the mixture into an 8-inch loaf pan that has been coated with nonstick vegetable spray; bake for 50 minutes. Spread the remaining 3 tablespoons barbecue sauce over the top and bake for 10 more minutes, or until the meat loaf is cooked through and the juices run clear.

NOTE: Change the taste each time you make this by using a different brand or flavor of barbecue sauce—smoky one time, zesty the next, and so on.

Tempting Turkey Tetrazzini

6 to 8 servings

Bet you can't say the name three times fast. And I also bet that you'll want at least three helpings! Now control yourself!

8 ounces uncooked spaghetti
1 can (14½ ounces) ready-to-use chicken broth
8 ounces fresh mushrooms, sliced (about 3 cups)
2 cups low-fat milk
3 tablespoons cornstarch

¼ cup dry white wine or water
3 cups coarsely chopped cooked turkey breast (about 1 pound)
½ teaspoon salt
½ teaspoon black pepper
¼ cup Italian-style bread crumbs

Preheat the oven to 375°F. Cook the spaghetti according to the package directions; drain and set aside. In a large saucepan, bring the broth to a boil over medium-high heat. Stir in the mushrooms, then reduce the heat to medium-low and simmer for 4 to 5 minutes, or until the mushrooms are tender. Stir in the milk. In a small cup, combine the cornstarch and wine and stir until smooth; slowly pour into the mushroom mixture. Increase the heat to medium and bring to a boil, stirring constantly. Remove from the heat and stir in the turkey, salt, and pepper. Add the spaghetti and toss until well coated. Spoon the spaghetti mixture into a 9" × 13" baking dish that has been coated with nonstick vegetable spray and sprinkle evenly with the bread crumbs. Bake for 20 to 25 minutes, or until golden and bubbly.

NOTE: Don't think that you have to roast a whole turkey to get the cooked turkey to make this. No, sir. Do what I do—buy a 1-pound chunk in the deli and cut it up yourself.

Turkey Barbecue Sandwich

4 servings

So you love turkey sandwiches, huh? So do I! But every so often I like to jazz them up, and this sandwich does it for me.

1 pound ground turkey breast
1 cup barbecue sauce
¼ cup mild salsa

4 hamburger buns, split and
     toasted

Coat a large skillet with nonstick vegetable spray. Add the turkey and brown over medium heat, stirring frequently to break it up. Reduce the heat to low and add the barbecue sauce and salsa; simmer until warmed through, about 5 to 7 minutes. Spoon the turkey mixture evenly over the toasted buns and serve immediately.

NOTE: Serve with Baked Sweet Potato Fries (page 234) to round out this different meal.

My Own Turkey Sausage

4 to 6 servings

Sausage you can make yourself? Well, why not? It's so easy! And since you control exactly what goes into it, you'll be able to watch the fat content while giving it exactly the tastes you want.

1 pound ground turkey breast
1 small onion, chopped
¼ cup egg substitute
2 tablespoons dry bread crumbs
1 teaspoon ground thyme

1 teaspoon fennel seed
½ teaspoon garlic powder
1 teaspoon salt
½ teaspoon black pepper
¼ teaspoon cayenne pepper

Combine all the ingredients in a large bowl; mix well. Form the mixture into 4 to 6 equal-sized patties. Coat a large nonstick skillet with nonstick vegetable spray. Place the patties in the skillet and cook over medium heat for 3 to 4 minutes per side, or until no pink remains in the center.

NOTE: Serve on buns with lettuce and tomatoes, or with lightly sautéed onions for that "I can't believe I made it myself!" sausage flavor.

Sicilian Turkey Meatballs

30 meatballs

Make these a day or two in advance. Then, when mealtime comes, you've got dinner in a snap!

1 pound ground turkey breast
1 pound Italian turkey sausage,
    casings removed
1½ cups shredded wheat cereal,
    crushed

2 egg whites
½ cup dry red wine
1 jar (28 ounces) light spaghetti
    sauce

In a large bowl, combine all the ingredients except the spaghetti sauce; mix well. Form into 1½-inch meatballs. Place the meatballs in a large saucepan and add the spaghetti sauce. Cover and cook over medium-low heat for 25 to 28 minutes, or until no pink remains in the meatballs.

NOTE: You can serve these over spaghetti or other pasta, or you can make a super turkey meatball sandwich. If you want, you can substitute ½ cup water for the ½ cup dry red wine.

Easy Turkey Chili

6 to 8 servings

If you're one of the people who still thinks that reducing fat and calories means reducing taste . . . I guarantee that this recipe will change your mind!

1 pound ground turkey breast
1 medium-sized onion, chopped
1 medium-sized green bell pepper, chopped
½ teaspoon minced garlic
3 cans (16 ounces each) navy beans, rinsed and drained

2 cans (14½ ounces each) whole tomatoes, coarsely chopped
1 cup salsa
2 tablespoons chili powder
1 teaspoon ground cumin
1 teaspoon salt
1 teaspoon black pepper

Coat a large saucepan with nonstick vegetable spray. Add the turkey, onion, bell pepper, and garlic. Cook over medium-high heat for 5 to 7 minutes, until no pink remains, stirring occasionally to break up the turkey. Add the remaining ingredients. Bring to a boil, stirring occasionally. Reduce the heat to low; cover and simmer for 20 minutes.

NOTE: For added flavor, chop some additional onion to sprinkle on top, or top each serving with a dollop of reduced-fat sour cream or your favorite shredded low-fat cheese.

Spicy Turkey Cassoulet

6 to 8 servings

The secret here is the spicy turkey sausage. Not only does it contain less fat than most other sausages, but it's full of spices that enhance the whole recipe. Why, I bet it'll qualify you as a real kitchen hero!

1 pound spicy turkey sausage, cut into ½-inch slices
1 cup uncooked orzo pasta
2 teaspoons minced garlic
2 cans (14½ ounces each) stewed tomatoes, undrained
1 can (16 to 19 ounces) cannellini or Great Northern beans, rinsed and drained

1 package (16 ounces) frozen mixed vegetables (broccoli, cauliflower, and carrots)
1½ cups water
1 teaspoon dried thyme
1 teaspoon salt
½ teaspoon black pepper

In a large saucepan, cook the sausage over medium heat for 10 to 12 minutes, until no pink remains. Add the orzo and garlic and stir constantly for 5 to 7 minutes, or until the orzo begins to brown. Add the remaining ingredients; stir gently, then cover and cook for 20 to 25 minutes, stirring occasionally.

NOTE: As always, there are no rules. You can certainly use any type of vegetable combination you've got on hand.

Turkey Pot Pie

6 to 8 servings

Frozen pot pies are often full of artificial flavors and preservatives. When you make them fresh at home, you can be sure you'll be serving only the best!

1 can (14½ ounces) reduced-
    sodium ready-to-use chicken
    broth
1 small onion, chopped
1 package (10 ounces) frozen peas
    and carrots, thawed
3 tablespoons cornstarch
1 can (12 ounces) evaporated
    skim milk
3 cups cubed cooked turkey breast
    (about 1 pound) (fresh-cooked
    or deli-style turkey)

¾ teaspoon ground sage
½ teaspoon dried parsley flakes
⅛ teaspoon black pepper
3 sheets (12" × 17" each) frozen
    phyllo dough (from a
    1-pound box), thawed
    (see Note)
Nonstick vegetable spray

Preheat the oven to 350°F. In a medium-sized saucepan, combine the broth, onions, and peas and carrots. Bring to a boil over medium-high heat; reduce the heat to low and simmer for 5 minutes. In a medium-sized bowl, combine the cornstarch and evaporated milk; stir until the cornstarch is dissolved. Slowly stir the milk mixture into the broth. Add the turkey, sage, parsley, and pepper. Continue cooking, stirring constantly, until the mixture has thickened. Pour into a 7" × 11" baking dish that has been coated with nonstick vegetable spray. Cut the sheets of phyllo dough in half crosswise. Place one sheet over the turkey mixture, tucking the edges down around the turkey mixture to seal completely. Coat the dough with nonstick baking spray. Repeat the layers until all of the phyllo dough is used. Bake for 40 to 45 minutes, or until the crust is golden brown.

NOTE: Allow the phyllo dough to thaw while still wrapped. Once it has thawed, remove 3 sheets from the package and cover them with a moistened cloth until ready to use, to keep them from drying out. Rewrap and refrigerate the remaining dough.

Tender Turkey Tips

4 servings

We've all heard of beef tenderloin tips. Well, that's what this dish tastes like, even though it's made with turkey breast!

1 teaspoon canola or
    vegetable oil
1 pound boneless, skinless turkey
    breast, cut into 1" × 2" strips
2 medium-sized onions, thinly
    sliced
8 ounces fresh mushrooms, sliced
    (about 3 cups)

½ cup water
¼ cup dry red wine
1½ teaspoons steak sauce
⅛ teaspoon dried thyme
½ teaspoon salt

In a large skillet, heat the oil over medium-high heat. Add the turkey and sauté for 4 to 5 minutes, or until lightly browned. Add the onions and mushrooms and cook for 2 to 3 minutes, or until the onions are tender. Reduce the heat to low and add the remaining ingredients; cook for 2 to 3 more minutes, or until heated through, stirring frequently.

NOTE: To make this a complete meal, serve it on a bed of warm curly no-yolk egg noodles or steamed white or brown rice.

Grilled Turkey and Pear Kebabs

4 kebabs

Do you have two pears? No, not as in playing cards, but for the main ingredient to share the skewers with the turkey breast!

Four 12-inch wooden or metal
    skewers
½ cup apple juice
⅓ cup light rum
¼ cup honey
¼ teaspoon ground cinnamon
2 medium-sized red bell peppers,
    cut into 1½-inch pieces

2 fresh pears, cored and cut into
    8 wedges each
1 pound boneless, skinless turkey
    breast cutlets, cut into
    1½-inch chunks
1 tablespoon cornstarch

If using wooden skewers, soak them in water for 15 to 20 minutes. Preheat the broiler. In a small bowl, combine the apple juice, rum, honey, and cinnamon; mix until thoroughly combined. Place ¾ cup of the mixture in a small saucepan and reserve the remaining mixture for basting the kebabs. On each skewer, thread alternating pieces of pepper, pear, and turkey, starting and ending with a piece of pepper. Broil the kebabs for 20 to 25 minutes, or until no pink remains in the turkey, basting every 5 minutes with the reserved honey mixture. Meanwhile, dissolve the cornstarch in the ¾ cup honey mixture and heat over medium heat for 3 to 4 minutes, or until thick and glossy. Remove from the heat. Drizzle the heated honey sauce over the kebabs.

Turkey Goulash

6 to 8 servings

If you're wondering why so many of these recipes call for ground turkey breast, it's because 3 to 4 ounces of it contain just a trace of fat, yet it's packed with protein.

2 pounds ground turkey breast
½ of a medium-sized green bell
    pepper, chopped
1 small onion, chopped
1 jar (28 ounces) light spaghetti
    sauce
8 ounces uncooked elbow
    macaroni

½ cup water
2 teaspoons garlic powder
1 teaspoon salt
½ teaspoon black pepper
½ cup (2 ounces) shredded
    reduced-fat mozzarella cheese

Preheat the oven to 350°F. In a large skillet, brown the ground turkey with the bell pepper and onion over medium-high heat for 6 to 8 minutes, or until no pink remains in the turkey. Drain off the excess liquid. Add the remaining ingredients except the cheese and stir to mix well. Place the mixture in a 2½-quart casserole dish that has been coated with nonstick vegetable spray. Cover and bake for 25 minutes. Remove from the oven and top with the cheese. Return to the oven and bake, uncovered, for 15 to 20 more minutes, until the cheese is melted and begins to brown.

Blackened Turkey Steaks

4 to 5 servings

Viewers often write in and ask why their turkey always tastes so bland. Well, turkey requires a lot of seasoning to really hold particular flavors. That's why I like preparing this Cajun-style turkey cutlet. What it lacks in fat (yeah!), it makes up for in flavor (yeah again!).

2 teaspoons paprika
1 teaspoon crushed dried thyme
½ teaspoon sugar
½ teaspoon onion powder
½ teaspoon garlic powder

½ teaspoon salt
½ teaspoon black pepper
¼ teaspoon cayenne pepper
1 to 1¼ pounds boneless, skinless
    turkey breast cutlets

In a small bowl, combine all the ingredients except the turkey; mix well. Rub the turkey cutlets well with the seasoning mixture. Heat a large nonstick skillet over high heat. Add the turkey and cook for 2 minutes per side, or until no pink remains and the juices run clear. Serve immediately.

Meat

Lean on your butcher! If you think you need to give up meat in your quest to eat lighter, you're wrong! Here are a few pointers that'll help you shop, prepare, and serve meats with moderation in mind:

- Know what you're buying. Look for lean ground meats—ones that are at least 85 percent lean.
- Keep your meats "mean and lean." Have your butcher trim the fat, leaving no more than ¼ inch visible fat. (You may want to trim it a bit more yourself before cooking.) You'll be trimming your grocery bill, too!
- Buy quality USDA Select meats, which are typically lean but still tender and flavorful.
- The main type of meat to avoid is any with noticeable heavy marbling. Yes, heavily marbled meats taste great, but they also contain more fat.
- Look for cuts of beef and veal that are marked "round" or "loin." They are typically leaner than other cuts.
- When cooking lighter with pork, I like to stick to cuts from the tenderloin and loin. I also use trimmed boneless ham.
- Loin chops and well-trimmed leg are the leanest lamb cuts.
- Limit consumption of organ meats such as liver, tongue, and sweetbreads. They're typically high in fat and cholesterol.
- Keep your portions under control! It's not necessary to serve a 12-ounce steak as a matter of course. It's actually recommended that portions be 3 to 4 ounces uncooked. That's about the size of a deck of playing cards.

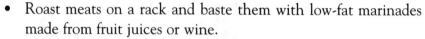

- Roast meats on a rack and baste them with low-fat marinades made from fruit juices or wine.
- Drain meat after browning it for one-pot dishes like stew and chili.
- After browning crumbled ground beef, remove it to a plate lined with white paper towels to drain off the excess fat; drain the cooking pan and return the meat to it to continue cooking. Another method is to remove the crumbled cooked ground beef to a colander and rinse it gently with hot tap water before adding seasonings and/or other ingredients.
- Instead of making thick gravy, remove the fat from the pan drippings and then simmer the drippings to make a rich, natural sauce.

Meat

Early-Bird Special

6 to 8 servings

In some areas of the country, if you go to a particular restaurant earlier than the main dinner hours, they'll offer special discounts and maybe even special meals. One of the most popular ones where I live in South Florida is a steak similar to this one.

One 2- to 2½-pound beef top round steak
1½ cups Burgundy or other dry red wine
1 can (10½ ounces) condensed French onion soup

1 tablespoon minced garlic
1 tablespoon sugar
2 teaspoons light soy sauce
¼ teaspoon ground ginger
2 tablespoons all-purpose flour
¼ cup water

Place the beef in a large resealable plastic storage bag and place open-end up in a deep bowl. In a medium-sized bowl, combine the wine, soup, garlic, sugar, soy sauce, and ginger; mix well. Pour over the beef in the bag and seal tightly. Refrigerate for 8 hours, or overnight, turning the bag occasionally to marinate evenly. Preheat the broiler. Remove the beef to a broiler pan or rimmed baking sheet that has been coated with nonstick vegetable spray, reserving the marinade. Broil the meat for 30 to 35 minutes for medium-rare, or to desired doneness, turning halfway through the cooking. Meanwhile, place the marinade in a small saucepan and bring to a boil over medium-high heat. In a small bowl, combine the flour and water; whisk until the flour is dissolved. Slowly add the flour mixture to the boiling marinade, then reduce the heat to medium-low and simmer for 3 to 4 minutes, or until the sauce thickens. Slice the meat across the grain and serve with the Burgundy onion sauce from the pan.

Oniony Salisbury Steaks

6 servings

When I was a kid, I could count on getting a great Salisbury steak at the local diner. I remember how it sizzled on the grill with loads of onions. Well, today's version is much lighter, since we start off with lean ground beef and bake it in the oven. Sure, we get the same great flavor, but so much lighter!

1½ pounds lean ground beef
3 egg whites
2 medium-sized onions, chopped, divided
¾ cup dry bread crumbs
½ cup low-fat milk
1 tablespoon dried Italian seasoning

1 teaspoon salt
1 can (10½ ounces) condensed beef broth
1 can (10¾ ounces) reduced-fat condensed cream of mushroom soup
¼ teaspoon garlic powder
¼ teaspoon black pepper

Preheat the oven to 350°F. In a large bowl, combine the ground beef, egg whites, half the chopped onions, the bread crumbs, milk, Italian seasoning, and salt; mix well. Shape the mixture into 6 equal-sized oval-shaped patties. Place the patties on a rimmed baking sheet that has been coated with nonstick vegetable spray and bake for 25 to 30 minutes, or until the juices run clear, turning halfway through the baking. In a medium-sized saucepan that has been coated with nonstick vegetable spray, sauté the remaining chopped onions for 3 to 4 minutes, or until tender. Add the remaining ingredients and stir until well combined. Simmer over medium-low heat for 8 to 10 minutes, or until warmed through. Remove the steaks to a serving platter and top with the sauce.

Crowd-Pleasing Roast

10 to 12 servings

You can have your beef and a healthier diet, too—just make sure you buy it right and prepare it right. If you haven't done so already, see my guide to eating lighter meats on pages 143 to 144.

One 4- to 5-pound beef eye of the round roast
1½ cups ketchup
⅓ cup prepared yellow mustard
½ cup firmly packed light brown sugar
2 tablespoons water

Preheat the oven to 325°F. Place the roast in a large roasting pan that has been coated with nonstick vegetable spray. In a medium-sized bowl, combine the remaining ingredients; mix well. Pour over the roast. Cover tightly with aluminum foil and bake for 2 to 2½ hours, until a meat thermometer inserted in the center reads 160°F. for medium, or to desired doneness. Slice the roast and serve with the pan juices.

Mean 'n' Lean Beef Stew

4 to 6 servings

You can still enjoy the great flavor of your old favorite beef stew, but now, by reducing the amount of beef and using even more vegetables, what you get to cut down on is fat and calories.

1 pound beef flank steak, well
    trimmed and cut into 1-inch
    cubes
¼ cup all-purpose flour
½ teaspoon garlic powder
½ teaspoon onion powder
½ teaspoon salt
½ teaspoon black pepper
1 medium-sized onion, cut into 8
    wedges

4 medium-sized carrots, cut into
    1-inch pieces
2 large celery stalks, cut into
    ½-inch slices
1 can (10½ ounces) condensed
    beef broth
5 medium-sized potatoes, cut into
    1-inch chunks

In a medium-sized bowl, combine the steak and flour; toss to coat well. Coat a nonstick soup pot with nonstick vegetable spray and heat over medium-high heat. Add the beef, then sprinkle with the garlic powder, onion powder, salt, and pepper. Sauté for 3 to 5 minutes, or until the steak is browned on all sides. Add the remaining ingredients except the potatoes; cover, reduce the heat to low, and simmer for 40 to 45 minutes. Add the potatoes; cover and simmer for 20 to 25 minutes, or until the potatoes are fork-tender.

Twin Pepper Steak Kebabs

8 kebabs

Most of today's meat cuts are leaner than they used to be. That's why I chose top sirloin for this—it's got the same big taste we always loved, but it's a little lighter now.

Eight 10- to 12-inch metal or wooden skewers
1 cup ketchup
¼ cup steak sauce
⅔ cup firmly packed light brown sugar
½ cup apple cider vinegar
2 tablespoons Worcestershire sauce

1½ to 2 pounds boneless beef top sirloin steak, well trimmed and cut into 32 equal-sized chunks
1 medium-sized green bell pepper, cut into 16 pieces
1 medium-sized red bell pepper, cut into 16 pieces

If using wooden skewers, soak them in water for 15 to 20 minutes. In a medium-sized saucepan, combine the ketchup, steak sauce, brown sugar, vinegar, and Worcestershire sauce over medium heat; bring to a boil, stirring occasionally until the sugar is dissolved. Remove from the heat and allow to cool. Thread each skewer alternately with pieces of steak and bell peppers so that there are 4 pieces of steak, 2 pieces of red bell pepper, and 2 pieces of green bell pepper on each. Place the skewers in a 9" × 13" glass baking dish and pour the cooled sauce over the top. Cover and chill for at least 2 hours, or overnight. Preheat the broiler. Place the kebabs on a rimmed baking sheet that has been coated with nonstick vegetable spray. Broil for 14 to 16 minutes, or to desired doneness, turning halfway through the cooking.

NOTE: These can also be cooked on a barbecue or an indoor grill for the same amount of time.

Simmerin' Beef One-Pot

6 to 8 servings

One-pot simmering means the stove does all the work and you get all the credit. Who wouldn't like that?!

¼ cup white vinegar
1 medium-sized onion, chopped
3 tablespoons dark brown sugar
1 teaspoon ground ginger
¼ teaspoon ground cloves
⅛ teaspoon ground allspice

2 teaspoons salt
½ teaspoon black pepper
3 cups water
One 2½- to 3-pound beef brisket, trimmed

In a soup pot, combine all the ingredients except the brisket; mix well. Add the brisket and bring to a boil over medium-high heat. Reduce the heat to low; cover and simmer for 2 hours, or until fork-tender. Remove the brisket from the pot; thinly slice across the grain and serve.

NOTE: If you'd like to give your brisket a glazed topping, check out the Chili Glaze on the next page.

Chili Glaze

¾ cup

Here's a way to turn Simmerin' Beef One-Pot into a tasty, saucy main dish simply by adding three "off-the-shelf" ingredients. (Of course, you can top your favorite pot roast with this, too.)

½ cup beer   2 tablespoons dark brown sugar
¼ cup chili sauce

Preheat the oven to 350°F. In a small bowl, combine all the ingredients; mix well. Place the whole cooked brisket in a 9" × 13" baking dish that has been coated with nonstick vegetable spray. Pour the sauce over the top and bake for 20 minutes, basting occasionally. Thinly slice across the grain, then pour the remaining glaze over the sliced brisket before serving.

Not-Your-Average Steak

5 to 6 servings

When I first put this together, everyone in my test kitchen thought I was crazy. I mean, the combination of ingredients looks a little strange. But it's really a great way to add flavor to a low-fat cut of meat. Oh, by the way, my staff loved it so much that they asked me to make it again and again!

1 can (14½ ounces) ready-to-use beef broth
½ cup dry red wine
½ cup raisins
¼ teaspoon ground cinnamon
One 1½- to 2-pound boneless beef top sirloin steak, well trimmed

2 tablespoons black peppercorns, crushed
2 tablespoons water
1 tablespoon cornstarch

Preheat the broiler. In a medium-sized saucepan, combine the broth, wine, raisins, and cinnamon over medium heat. Simmer for 20 to 25 minutes, until the liquid is reduced by half. Meanwhile, sprinkle both sides of the steak with the peppercorns. With a kitchen mallet, pound the peppercorns into the meat. Place the steak on a broiler pan or baking sheet that has been coated with nonstick vegetable spray and broil for 8 minutes, for medium, or to desired doneness, turning halfway through the cooking. In a small bowl, combine the water and cornstarch; stir until smooth. Slowly add to the reduced broth mixture, stirring until thickened. Thinly slice the steak across the grain and serve immediately, topped with the sauce.

NOTE: You can use coarse-ground pepper if you don't have whole peppercorns.

Italian Cubed Steak

4 servings

Looking for a different way with cubed steak? Try it Italian style! Even with no added fat, the taste is . . . how do they say it? *Magnifico!*

¼ cup all-purpose flour
½ teaspoon paprika
¼ teaspoon black pepper
Four 6-ounce beef cubed steaks
1 cup condensed beef broth

1 can (8 ounces) Italian-style
    stewed tomatoes, undrained
1 teaspoon garlic powder
¼ cup water
2 tablespoons cornstarch

In a shallow dish, combine the flour, paprika, and pepper; add the steaks and turn to coat lightly. Coat a large skillet with nonstick vegetable spray and heat over medium-high heat. Cook the steaks for 10 to 14 minutes, turning halfway through the cooking. Remove the steaks to a platter and cover to keep warm. Reduce the heat to medium and add the broth, stewed tomatoes, and garlic powder to the skillet. Heat, stirring occasionally, just until the mixture begins to boil. In a small bowl, combine the water and cornstarch; stir until smooth. Slowly add to the tomato mixture and stir until thickened and smooth. Return the steaks to the pan and cook until thoroughly heated. Serve immediately.

Jalapeño-Studded Garlic Roast

8 to 10 servings

We usually put the seasoning on the outside of a roast, but this one has the seasoning baked inside the meat for an extra burst of flavor.

One 3- to 3½-pound beef eye of the round roast
2 tablespoons chopped jalapeño peppers
20 garlic cloves
2 teaspoons salt

¼ teaspoon cayenne pepper
1 can (14½ ounces) ready-to-use beef broth
6 scallions, chopped
3 tablespoons cornstarch

Preheat the oven to 350°F. With a sharp paring knife, carefully pierce the surface of the roast evenly 20 times, making each slit about 1½ inches deep. Stuff the jalapeño peppers evenly into the cuts, then place a garlic clove in each cut. Rub the roast all over with the salt and cayenne pepper. Coat a large oven-proof pot with

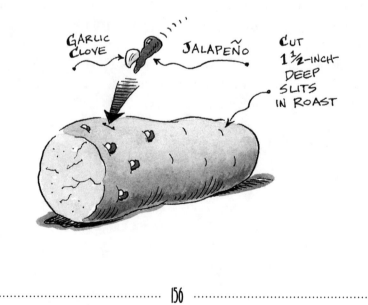

GARLIC CLOVE   JALAPEÑO   CUT 1½-INCH DEEP SLITS IN ROAST

nonstick vegetable spray and heat over medium heat. Place the roast in the pot and cook for 8 to 10 minutes, or until browned all over. Add the broth and scallions; cover and bake for 1 to 1¼ hours, until a meat thermometer inserted in the center of the roast registers 160°F. for medium, or to desired doneness. Remove the roast to a cutting board; skim and discard the fat from the pan juices. In a small bowl, combine the cornstarch and ½ cup of the pan juices. Return the cornstarch mixture to the pot and simmer over medium heat for 3 to 5 minutes, or until thickened. Slice the roast and place the slices on a serving platter. Pour the sauce over the top and serve.

So-Light Beef Stroganoff

6 to 8 servings

Beef Stroganoff has always been one of my favorites and, yes, in this case its European roots do mean that it was originally high in fat. Well, we can celebrate now because my new version is much lower in fat, but still has that fabulous Continental flavor.

1½ pounds boneless beef top sirloin steak, well trimmed and thinly sliced across the grain
1 small onion, chopped
8 ounces fresh mushrooms, sliced
1 can (10¾ ounces) reduced-fat condensed cream of mushroom soup

1 cup dry white wine
⅛ teaspoon white pepper
1 pound uncooked no-yolk egg noodles
½ cup reduced-fat sour cream
2 tablespoons chopped fresh parsley

In a nonstick skillet that has been coated with nonstick vegetable spray, brown the beef and onions over medium-high heat for 5 to 7 minutes, or until no pink remains in the steak and the onions are tender, stirring occasionally. Add the mushrooms and cook for 3 minutes, or until tender. Reduce the heat to medium-low and stir in the soup, wine, and pepper; simmer for 25 minutes, or until the meat is tender. Prepare the noodles according to the package directions; drain, rinse, and drain again, then set aside, covered, to keep warm. Add the sour cream and parsley to the soup mixture, and cook for 1 minute, or until heated through; do not boil. Serve over the warm noodles.

NOTE: If you prefer a saltier flavor, as I do, then add ½ teaspoon salt when you add the pepper.

Chinese Sirloin Steak

4 to 6 servings

If you've heard that beef doesn't fit in with today's diets, think again! When selected and prepared properly, it's today's smart choice.

1 can (10½ ounces) condensed
   beef broth
4 garlic cloves, minced
¼ cup ketchup
¼ cup honey

¼ cup soy sauce
One 2- to 2¼-pound boneless
   beef top sirloin steak, about
   1 inch thick, well trimmed

In a medium-sized bowl, combine all the ingredients except the steak. Place the steak in a 9" × 13" glass baking dish and cover with the marinade. Cover and refrigerate for at least 4 hours, or overnight, turning occasionally. Preheat the broiler. Place the steak on a broiler pan or rimmed baking sheet; discard the marinade. Broil for 14 to 16 minutes, for medium-rare, or to desired doneness, turning halfway through the cooking. Thinly slice across the grain and serve immediately.

NOTE: The longer this marinates, the more flavor will be absorbed by the steak. So, for best flavor, marinate overnight.

Barbecued Beef Hoagies

8 servings

I've added lots of mushrooms and onions to my regular barbecued beef, which not only makes it go farther, it lightens it up at the same time.

1 tablespoon canola or
  vegetable oil
4 large onions, thinly sliced
10 ounces fresh mushrooms,
  sliced
2 pounds lean beef top round,
  thinly sliced

½ cup chili sauce
½ cup ketchup
½ teaspoon salt
½ teaspoon black pepper
8 Italian-style hoagie rolls, sliced
  ¾ through

In a large nonstick skillet, heat the oil over medium-high heat; add the onions and sauté for 3 to 4 minutes, or until tender. Add the mushrooms and sauté for 3 to 4 more minutes, or until the mushrooms are tender and the onions begin to brown, stirring occasionally. Remove the vegetables to a bowl. In the same skillet, brown the steak over medium-high heat for 6 to 7 minutes, or until no pink remains; drain off any excess liquid. Return the vegetables to the skillet and add the chili sauce, ketchup, salt, and pepper. Cook for 3 to 4 minutes, or until thoroughly heated, stirring occasionally. Spoon into the hoagie rolls and serve immediately.

NOTE: Ask your butcher to cut the meat nice and thin. I started out as a butcher, so I know it'll be his or her pleasure!

Beefy Fried Rice

4 to 6 servings

This is a real meal-in-one that you can have ready for your gang in just minutes. It's perfect for when you're in a rush, or any time you don't want to spend all evening cooking!

1 pound lean ground beef
2 garlic cloves, minced
¼ teaspoon ground ginger
2 tablespoons water
1 medium-sized red bell pepper,
   cut into ½-inch chunks

1 package (6 ounces) frozen pea
   pods, thawed
3 cups cold cooked rice
3 tablespoons soy sauce
2 teaspoons sesame oil
2 scallions, thinly sliced

In a large nonstick skillet, combine the ground beef, garlic, and ginger over medium heat; cook, stirring to break up the beef, for 8 to 10 minutes, or until no pink remains in the beef. Drain off the excess liquid and remove the beef to a large bowl. Add the water to the skillet and heat over medium-high heat until hot; add the bell pepper and pea pods and cook for 3 minutes, or until the pepper is crisp-tender, stirring occasionally. Add the rice, soy sauce, and sesame oil; mix well. Return the beef to the skillet and cook for 5 minutes, or until heated through. Stir in the scallions and serve.

"Souper" Sloppy Joes

6 servings

You've heard of Sloppy Joes . . . well, I've "souped" them up! And not only are they "souper" now . . . they're *super,* too.

1 pound lean ground beef
1 small onion, chopped
1 can (10¾ ounces) reduced-fat
   condensed cream of
   mushroom soup
1 tablespoon prepared yellow
   mustard

1 tablespoon ketchup
½ teaspoon browning and
   seasoning sauce
⅛ teaspoon black pepper
6 hamburger buns, split and
   toasted

In a large skillet, cook the ground beef and onion over medium heat until the onion is tender and the beef is browned, stirring often to break up the beef. Drain off the excess liquid, then stir in the remaining ingredients except the buns. Reduce the heat to medium-low and cook for 5 to 8 minutes, or until heated through, stirring occasionally. Serve on the buns.

NOTE: These can also be served over regular toast or toasted Italian bread as open-faced sandwiches.

Porcupine Meatballs

6 to 8 servings

Whether the name scares you or makes you curious, you've got to try these! It's the rice sticking out the sides of the meatballs that makes us call them porcupines.

2 cans (8 ounces each) tomato
    sauce
3 tablespoons sugar
1½ pounds lean ground beef
1 egg
⅓ cup uncooked long- or
    whole-grain rice

3 tablespoons chopped onion
½ teaspoon salt
¼ teaspoon black pepper
1½ teaspoons Worcestershire
    sauce

In a medium-sized bowl, combine the tomato sauce and sugar. In a large bowl, combine the ground beef, egg, rice, onion, salt, pepper, and ⅓ cup of the tomato sauce mixture; mix well. Roll into 1-inch balls. Place in a large skillet and brown over medium-high heat for 7 to 8 minutes, or until browned on all sides. Stir the Worcestershire sauce into the remaining tomato sauce, then pour over the meatballs. Reduce the heat to low, cover, and cook for 30 to 35 minutes, or until the meatballs are cooked through and the rice is tender.

NOTE: Be sure that you don't use instant rice here.

Meat Loaf Muffins

12 muffins

Don't think that all ground beef is the same. This is an old favorite that I lightened up by using ground beef that has a meat-to-fat ratio of 90 to 10, which means that it's just 10% fat. If you need help with all the ground meat choices, ask your butcher.

2 pounds lean ground beef	1 cup dry bread crumbs
1 medium-sized zucchini, shredded	1 teaspoon dried Italian seasoning
	½ teaspoon salt
2 egg whites	½ cup barbecue sauce, divided

Preheat the oven to 400°F. In a large bowl, combine all the ingredients except ¼ cup barbecue sauce; mix lightly but thoroughly. Divide the beef mixture equally among the cups of a 12-cup muffin pan that has been coated with nonstick vegetable spray; smooth the tops. Spread the remaining barbecue sauce over the tops. Bake for 25 to 30 minutes, or until no pink remains and the juices run clear.

Veal Paprikash

4 to 6 servings

In my original paprikash recipe, I sautéed the meat in butter and oil. Here I eliminate them and brown the meat in a nonstick skillet. The tastes from the vegetables and spices keep this one a real winner!

1½ pounds veal stew meat, well trimmed and cut into 1-inch cubes

6 medium-sized onions, chopped

8 ounces fresh mushrooms, sliced (about 3 cups)

1 can (14½ ounces) whole tomatoes, undrained

1 bay leaf

2 teaspoons paprika

1 teaspoon salt

½ teaspoon black pepper

In a nonstick soup pot, brown the veal over high heat; drain off any excess liquid. Add the onions and mushrooms, reduce the heat to medium, and cook for 5 minutes, or until the onions are tender. Add the tomatoes and their juice, the bay leaf, paprika, salt, and pepper. Cover and reduce the heat to low; simmer for 45 minutes, or until the meat is tender. **Be sure to remove the bay leaf before serving.**

NOTE: Serve this over warm cooked noodles for an all-in-one meal.

Very Special Veal

4 servings

The name says it all—but it's simple enough to make even when you're pressed for time. That's why at my house it's nicknamed "V.S.V."

¼ cup all-purpose flour
1 pound boneless veal cutlets, pounded to ¼-inch thickness
2 teaspoons canola or vegetable oil, plus extra if needed
1 can (14½ ounces) ready-to-use chicken broth

1 can (14½ ounces) sliced carrots, drained
⅓ cup chopped scallions
1 can (14½ ounces) artichoke hearts, drained and quartered
½ teaspoon black pepper

Place the flour in a shallow dish; add the veal and turn to coat completely. In a large skillet, heat the oil over medium-high heat. Add the veal cutlets, a few at a time, and cook for 4 minutes, or until browned, turning halfway through the cooking. Remove the cooked veal to a plate. If necessary, add additional oil to the skillet, and cook the remaining cutlets. Place all the cooked cutlets back in the skillet and add the remaining ingredients; stir and bring to a boil. Cover and reduce the heat to medium-low. Simmer for 5 minutes, or until heated through.

Fruity Pork Loin

6 to 8 servings

Wait till you try this change of pace from your usual savory pork roast. It's got a fruity flavor 'cause it's stuffed with fruit. Boy, will you love it.

One 2½- to 3-pound center-cut single pork loin, well trimmed
12 dried pitted prunes

12 dried apricots
½ teaspoon salt
¼ teaspoon black pepper
3 tablespoons apricot preserves

Preheat the oven to 350°F. With a long thin knife, carefully make a horizontal slit lengthwise through the center of the roast. Twist the knife gently to make a ½-inch hole, making a "tunnel." Stuff the prunes and apricots alternately into the tunnel. Coat a roasting rack and roasting pan with nonstick vegetable spray. Place the pork on the rack in the pan. Sprinkle with the salt and pepper; cover tightly with aluminum foil. Bake for 1 hour.

Remove from the oven and spread the apricot preserves evenly over the top of the roast. Return to the oven and bake, uncovered, for 15 to 20 minutes, or until no pink remains. Remove the pork to a cutting board and slice across the grain. Serve immediately.

COME ON IN!

THE PORK!

THE PRUNES

THE APRICOTS

Pork Roast Marsala

6 to 8 servings

Make this the day before you plan to eat it—it takes just minutes to put together. Then all you have to do is warm it up . . . and enjoy it!

1 tablespoon canola or
vegetable oil
One 3-pound center-cut single
pork loin, well trimmed
8 ounces fresh mushrooms,
chopped (about 3 cups)
1 medium-sized onion, chopped
2 teaspoons minced garlic

1 can (10½ ounces) condensed
chicken broth
¾ cup Marsala wine
1 small tomato, chopped
½ teaspoon dried thyme
¼ cup water
2 tablespoons cornstarch

Heat the oil in a soup pot over medium heat. Add the pork and brown on all sides; discard the excess liquid. Add the mushrooms, onion, and garlic; cook for 6 to 8 minutes, stirring occasionally, or until the onions are tender. Stir in the chicken broth, wine, tomato, and thyme; bring to a boil, then cover and cook for 30 to 40 minutes, or until the pork juices run clear. Remove the pork to a cutting board. In a small bowl, combine the water and cornstarch; mix until smooth. Add to the sauce, stirring until thickened and well combined. Slice the pork into ¼-inch slices and place on a serving platter. Pour the sauce over the slices and serve.

NOTE: Marsala wine is readily available, but if you want you could use your favorite type of wine (except sweet) instead.

Honey-Garlic Pork Chops

4 servings

Everybody always says that all of the flavor of meat is in the fat. I say, "Phooey!" Because if we marinate it, we can still get big flavor. And when we marinate without oil, it's even better for us. Oh yeah, this one'll get you loads of oohs and aahs.

¾ cup lemon juice
¾ cup honey
⅓ cup soy sauce
¼ cup dry white wine

2 tablespoons minced garlic
4 pork loin chops (about 2 pounds total), ¾ inch thick, well trimmed

In a medium-sized bowl, combine all the ingredients except the pork chops; mix well. Place the chops in a 9" × 13" baking dish; pour the marinade over them. Cover and refrigerate for at least 4 hours, or overnight. Preheat the broiler. Remove the chops to a broiler pan that has been coated with nonstick vegetable spray; reserve the marinade. Broil the chops for 16 to 18 minutes, for medium-well, or to desired doneness, turning halfway through the broiling. Meanwhile, place the reserved marinade in a small saucepan and bring to a boil over medium-high heat. Reduce the heat to low; keep warm. Place the chops on a serving platter and top with the warm sauce. Serve immediately.

Peppered Pork Chops

4 servings

Pork used to be thought of as a very fatty meat, but with today's breeding and processing methods, the meat comes to us less fatty. Then we can trim off whatever fat remains and really enjoy pork while watching our fat and calories.

4 pork loin chops (about 2
   pounds total), ½ inch thick,
   well trimmed
1 small onion, finely chopped
1 teaspoon minced garlic
1 can (14½ ounces) ready-to-use
   chicken broth
¼ cup dry red wine (optional)
1 teaspoon lemon juice
1 tablespoon cornstarch
1 tablespoon crushed black
   peppercorns
½ teaspoon salt

Preheat the broiler. Place the chops on a broiler pan that has been coated with nonstick vegetable spray. Broil for 12 to 15 minutes, for medium-well, or until the chops are cooked to desired doneness beyond that, turning halfway through the cooking. Meanwhile, in a medium-sized nonstick skillet that has been coated with nonstick vegetable spray, sauté the onion and garlic over medium heat for 5 to 7 minutes, or until lightly browned. Add the remaining ingredients; cook, stirring, for 6 to 8 minutes, or until thickened. Place the pork chops on a serving platter; spoon the onion mixture evenly over the chops and serve immediately.

NOTE: To crush the peppercorns, place them in a plastic storage bag and crush gently with a mallet or rolling pin.

Country Pork Loaf

6 to 8 servings

It's in the beans. Yup, the secret to making this so good for us is in extending the pork by adding a can of beans. They're full of protein and fiber, and they offer us a refreshing change from all-meat meat loaf.

1 pound lean ground pork	1 teaspoon salt
1 cup dry bread crumbs	½ teaspoon black pepper
2 egg whites	1 can (16 to 19 ounces) Great
1 can (14½ ounces) stewed	Northern beans, rinsed and
tomatoes, drained	drained
1 teaspoon garlic powder	¼ cup ketchup

Preheat the oven to 375°F. In a large bowl, combine all the ingredients except the beans and ketchup; mix well. Gently stir in the beans, being careful not to break them up. Place the meat mixture in a 9" × 5" loaf pan that has been coated with nonstick vegetable spray. Spoon the ketchup over the loaf and spread evenly over the top. Bake for 60 to 65 minutes, or until the loaf is cooked through and the juices run clear.

Jamaican Pork Tenderloin

4 to 6 servings

Here's a light island favorite. It's simple, and the combination of lime and honey makes it oh so tasty!

¼ cup honey
⅓ cup lime juice
1 teaspoon grated lime zest
2 garlic cloves, minced
2 tablespoons prepared yellow
    mustard

½ teaspoon salt
½ teaspoon black pepper
2 pounds pork tenderloin
    (2 tenderloins), well
    trimmed

In a small bowl, combine all the ingredients except the tenderloin; mix well. Place the pork in a 7" × 11" glass baking dish and cover with the marinade. Cover and refrigerate for at least 4 hours, or overnight. Preheat the broiler. Place the pork on a broiler pan or rimmed baking sheet; discard the marinade. Broil for 14 to 16 minutes, or until no pink remains, turning halfway through the cooking. Slice across the grain and serve immediately.

Fish & Seafood

Fish and Seafood

Seafood is "catching" on! And why not? With better-than-ever processing and transportation methods, there are countless varieties of seafood available to us. It cooks quickly and, when it comes to keeping your diet under control, fish and seafood can really help. So make seafood part of your weekly meal planning.

All seafood is not the same when it comes to what it does for us, but if you follow these tips, before you know it, you'll be hooked on seafood . . . for good!

- Fresh, fresh, fresh! It's important to buy seafood that's fresh, no matter what kind it is. Also, don't keep it in your refrigerator for more than a day or two. Now when I say fresh, that includes fish that is quick-frozen. (It thaws in no time.) Quick-frozen fish is frozen almost immediately after being caught, making it fresher than some that hasn't been frozen and has undergone days of shipping.
- Purchase fish that has been stored under refrigeration or packed in ice, *not* soaked in water. If you have any questions, don't hesitate to ask your fish salesperson.
- Fresh fish should be firm to the touch, not mushy, and should not smell fishy.
- If you buy whole fish, it should be bright in color and the eyes should be clear and glossy (not sunken).
- Most fish can be "lightened up" by removing the skin before or after cooking and also by removing any visible fat after cooking.
- Always wash clams, mussels, and oysters well in cold water before cooking and discard any that do not open during cooking.

Mussels need special attention before cooking, so see my note on page 192 before buying and/or preparing them.

- Dark, firm fish, such as tuna and swordfish, contains higher levels of fat than white-fleshed fish, such as whiting, cod, and halibut. They're all a great source of protein, though.
- Shellfish is relatively low in fat. Clams, scallops, and mussels are recommended over lobster and shrimp because they're lower in fat and cholesterol. And don't be tempted to smother them in a load of butter—use moderation. Add flavor with herbs and spices and a squeeze or two of fresh lemon or lime.
- Avoid deep-frying, and, if sautéing, use a nonstick skillet with nonstick vegetable spray or minimal fat. It's better to broil, grill, poach, or "oven-fry" fish and other seafood. Check out "Oven-Fried" Fish (page 179). "Oven-frying" is a great option if you want to avoid the heavy smell that is thought of as typical of frying fish—and it makes cleanup a breeze, too.
- Canned fish that's packed in oil has much more fat than that packed in water, so choose water-packed every time.

Fish and Seafood

"Oven-Fried" Fish

4 to 6 servings

There's no reason we all can't enjoy Friday night fried fish flavor just because we're watching what we eat. "Oven-frying" is the answer!

1 egg white, beaten
½ teaspoon dried dillweed
½ teaspoon salt
½ teaspoon black pepper
1 cup cornflake crumbs

2 pounds fresh or frozen white-fleshed fish fillets, such as cod, haddock, or whiting, thawed if frozen, cut into 3-inch pieces
Nonstick vegetable spray

Preheat the oven to 400°F. In a shallow bowl, combine the egg white, dillweed, salt, and pepper. Place the cornflake crumbs in another shallow bowl. Dip the fish in the egg mixture, then in the crumbs, coating evenly. Place the fish on baking sheets that have been coated with nonstick vegetable spray. Coat the fish with nonstick vegetable spray and bake for 20 minutes, or until the fish flakes easily with a fork.

NOTE: Besides cutting down on fat, skipping the deep-frying by making it this way usually cuts down on the fishy smell that often hangs around the kitchen.

Sea Bass Florentine

4 to 6 servings

You're gonna really like this since it's practically fat-free *and* it's your main course and vegetables all cooked in one dish—making cleanup a breeze!

3 medium-sized carrots, peeled
    and julienned (see Note)
1 pound sea bass fillets, rinsed
    and patted dry
½ teaspoon salt
¼ teaspoon black pepper

1 lemon, cut in half
1 package (10 ounces) fresh
    spinach, washed and stems
    removed
1 can (5.5 ounces) vegetable
    juice

Preheat the oven to 375°F. Spread half of the carrots evenly over the bottom of a 9" × 13" glass baking dish. Place the fish fillets over the carrots in a single layer and sprinkle with the salt and pepper. Squeeze a lemon half over the fish, then place the spinach over the fish and squeeze the other lemon half over the spinach. Top with the remaining carrots. Pour the vegetable juice over the pan and cover with aluminum foil. Bake for 30 to 35 minutes, or until the fish flakes easily with a fork.

NOTE: Julienne-cut carrots are about the size of matchsticks. Try it. It looks fancy.

Pacific Fillets

4 to 6 servings

Most people shy away from cooking fish at home because they think it's difficult. That's definitely not true! As a matter of fact, this one's so easy you'll feel guilty when you hear all the compliments!

1 medium-sized onion, cut in half
   and sliced
1 can (14½ ounces) stewed
   tomatoes, undrained
⅓ cup dry red wine
3 tablespoons lemon juice

1 teaspoon ground cumin
⅛ teaspoon ground cinnamon
¼ cup sliced green salad olives
   (optional)
1 to 1½ pounds perch or red
   snapper fillets (about 6 fillets)

Preheat the oven to 400°F. Coat a large nonstick skillet with non-stick vegetable spray and heat over medium-high heat. Add the onion and cook for 3 to 4 minutes, or until tender, stirring constantly. Add the tomatoes, wine, lemon juice, cumin, and cinnamon; mix well. Cook for 5 to 7 minutes, stirring occasionally, until slightly thickened. Stir in the olives, if desired. Place the fish in a single layer in a 9" × 13" glass baking dish that has been coated with nonstick vegetable spray. Spoon the tomato mixture evenly over the top and cover tightly with aluminum foil. Bake for 15 to 20 minutes, or until the fish flakes easily with a fork.

Spicy Blackened Fish

4 servings

Get out your bookmark and mark this page. I just know that once you taste this, you'll be anxious to make it again and again.

1 teaspoon salt
1 teaspoon black pepper
¼ teaspoon cayenne pepper
¼ teaspoon paprika

¼ teaspoon garlic powder
1 pound mahi mahi, halibut, or
   swordfish steaks, skin
   removed

In a small bowl, combine the salt, black and cayenne peppers, paprika, and garlic powder; mix well. Rub evenly over both sides of the fish. Preheat a large nonstick skillet over medium-high heat. When hot, remove from the heat and coat with nonstick vegetable spray. Return to the heat, add the fish, and cook for 8 to 10 minutes, or until the fish is cooked through and flakes easily with a fork, turning halfway through the cooking.

NOTE: Most Cajun-style food is spicy-hot, and this dish is no exception, so be prepared! If you want to enjoy it in a less spicy version, try cutting the amount of black and cayenne peppers by half.

Apricot Mango Fillets

4 servings

No need to get out the tartar sauce or ketchup to top these fish fillets. That's 'cause I've spruced them up with a burst of fruit. Yeah . . . fruit!

1 pound fresh or frozen white-
  fleshed fish fillets, such as
  cod, haddock, or whiting,
  thawed if frozen
½ teaspoon salt, divided
1 can (16 ounces) apricot halves,
  drained

1 tablespoon light brown sugar
¼ teaspoon cayenne pepper
1 mango, peeled, pitted, and
  chopped

Preheat the broiler. Place the fish fillets on a broiler pan or rimmed baking sheet that has been coated with nonstick vegetable spray. Sprinkle evenly with ¼ teaspoon salt and broil for 5 minutes. Meanwhile, in a blender, combine the remaining ¼ teaspoon salt, the apricot halves, brown sugar, and cayenne pepper; blend on medium speed until a chunky purée forms. Pour the mixture into a small bowl and add the chopped mango; mix well. Spoon over the fish and broil for 4 to 6 minutes, or until the fish flakes easily with a fork and the sauce is hot and bubbly. Serve immediately.

NOTE: Papaya makes a good substitute for mango, but if no tropical fruits are available, 2 fresh peaches will work just as well.

Seafood Roll-ups

8 servings

A little of this, a little of that, and you'll have a double seafood sensation to surprise your gang.

½ pound imitation crabmeat
2 egg whites
½ cup finely crushed saltine crackers
¼ cup finely chopped onion
2 teaspoons minced garlic
1 medium-sized green bell pepper, finely chopped, divided

8 fresh or frozen white-fleshed fish fillets, such as cod, haddock, or whiting (3 to 4 ounces each), thawed if frozen
1 teaspoon salt
½ teaspoon black pepper
1 tablespoon lemon juice
½ teaspoon paprika
Nonstick vegetable spray

Preheat the oven to 400°F. In a medium-sized bowl, combine the crabmeat, egg whites, cracker crumbs, onion, garlic, and ¼ cup bell pepper; mix well. Place the fillets on a flat surface and sprinkle with the salt and pepper. Divide the crab mixture evenly over the fillets, then roll up. Place the roll-ups seam side down in a 7" × 11" glass baking dish that has been coated with nonstick vegetable spray. Sprinkle evenly with the lemon juice, paprika, and the remaining chopped bell pepper. Spray with nonstick vegetable spray and bake for 20 to 25 minutes, or until the fish flakes easily with a fork.

NOTE: If your fish fillets have skin, place the filling on the skin side and roll up. That way the skin will be on the inside of the roll-ups.

Baked Ranch Scallops

4 to 6 servings

Three simple ingredients add up to big taste. Why, just watch them come running when you ring that dinner bell!

1 envelope (1 ounce) ranch salad
   dressing mix

½ cup dry bread crumbs
1 pound bay scallops, rinsed

Preheat the oven to 350°F. In a large resealable plastic storage bag, combine the ranch dressing mix and bread crumbs; seal and shake to mix. Add the scallops and toss to coat. Place the scallops in a single layer in an 8-inch square glass baking dish that has been coated with nonstick vegetable spray and bake for 13 to 16 minutes, or until the outsides are golden and the insides are firm and white.

NOTE: Bay or sea scallops will work fine here. I prefer the smaller bay scallops because I think they're sweeter. Oh, if you do use sea scallops, add an additional 5 minutes to the baking time.

Restaurant-Style Shrimp Scampi

4 to 6 servings

Fourteen ninety-five? Seventeen ninety-five? Nineteen fifty? These are prices you might expect to pay at a nice restaurant for shrimp scampi. But look how simple it is to make at home (and you get to keep some of that savings in your pocket).

1 pound uncooked linguine
2 tablespoons olive oil
1 pound medium-sized shrimp, peeled, with tails left on and deveined
12 garlic cloves, crushed

1 teaspoon salt
½ teaspoon black pepper
½ cup dry white wine
2 tablespoons chopped fresh parsley

Cook the linguine according to the package directions; drain, rinse, drain again, and cover to keep warm. Meanwhile, in a large skillet, heat the oil over medium-high heat. Add the shrimp, garlic, salt, and pepper and sauté for 2 to 3 minutes, until the shrimp turns pink and is cooked through. Reduce the heat to low and add the wine and parsley; simmer for 1 to 2 minutes. Toss the shrimp with the linguine and serve immediately.

NOTE: Gee, I almost forgot to remind you to give the shrimp a squeeze of fresh lemon right before tossing with the pasta!

Mardi Gras Jambalaya

6 to 8 servings

All right, pretend it's Mardi Gras. Throw all these ingredients in one pot and crank up your favorite New Orleans jazz. That's the way to turn regular old dinner into a celebration!

1 pound fresh or frozen white-fleshed fish fillets, such as cod, haddock, or whiting, thawed if frozen, cut into 1-inch chunks

1 pound smoked turkey sausage, casings removed and cut into ½-inch slices

½ pound medium-sized shrimp, peeled and deveined

1 can (28 ounces) crushed tomatoes, undrained

1 can (14½ ounces) ready-to-use chicken broth

1 cup uncooked long- or whole-grain rice

½ cup dry white wine

2 medium-sized green or red bell peppers, coarsely chopped

1 large onion, coarsely chopped

4 teaspoons Creole seasoning

1 teaspoon garlic powder

Combine all the ingredients in a soup pot over medium heat; mix well. Cover and cook for 15 minutes. Reduce the heat to low and simmer for 30 to 35 minutes, or until the rice is cooked.

NOTE: If you've got them, use 1 green and 1 red bell pepper. (In case you hadn't guessed, I like to make my food as colorful as possible!)

One-Cook Paella

6 to 8 servings

You can cook just once and have the option to make dinner for tonight and tomorrow, or dinner for tonight and lunch for tomorrow, or dinner for tonight and a frozen dinner for another night. So many choices!

½ pound turkey sausage, cut into ½-inch-thick slices
1 medium-sized onion, chopped
1 medium-sized red bell pepper, cut into thin strips
3 garlic cloves, minced
1 teaspoon dried thyme
2 cups uncooked long- or whole-grain rice

1 can (14½ ounces) ready-to-use chicken broth
1 can (14½ ounces) diced tomatoes, undrained
2 bottles (8 ounces each) clam juice
½ teaspoon ground turmeric
½ pound medium-sized shrimp, peeled and deveined

In a large pot that has been coated with nonstick vegetable spray, brown the sausage over medium heat, 4 to 5 minutes. Add the onion, bell pepper, garlic, and thyme; cook for 3 to 5 minutes, or until the vegetables are tender. Add the rice, broth, tomatoes and their juice, the clam juice, and turmeric; mix well. Bring to a boil, then reduce the heat to low, cover, and simmer for 25 minutes. Stir in the shrimp and cook for 5 minutes, or until the shrimp are pink and cooked through, the rice is tender, and no liquid remains.

Shrimp 'n' Pasta

4 servings

By teaming our favorite shrimp with pasta, we can have something special and still stretch our food dollars. Of course, that's also a great way to make our dinner guests feel important!

8 ounces uncooked rigatoni or
   other medium pasta shape
1 pound medium-sized shrimp,
   peeled and deveined
1 medium-sized green bell pepper,
   cut into thin strips
1 medium-sized red bell pepper,
   cut into thin strips

1 cup sliced fresh mushrooms
3 garlic cloves, minced
1 tablespoon dried basil
2 medium-sized tomatoes,
   coarsely chopped
1 cup picante sauce

Cook the pasta according to the package directions; drain, rinse, drain again, and keep warm in a large bowl. Meanwhile, place the shrimp, peppers, mushrooms, garlic, and basil in a large nonstick skillet that has been coated with nonstick vegetable spray. Cook for 4 to 6 minutes over medium-high heat, until the shrimp are pink and cooked through and the peppers are almost tender, stirring frequently. Reduce the heat to low and stir in the tomatoes and picante sauce; simmer for 4 to 5 minutes, or until warmed through, stirring frequently. Add to the cooked pasta and toss to mix well.

NOTE: This dish can be as mild or as spicy as you please, depending on the picante sauce you choose.

Seafood One-Pot

8 servings

If you're a seafood lover, roll up your sleeves, grab a loaf of crusty bread and a big bowl and spoon, and you'll be "in business," as we always said.

1 pound cooked shrimp, peeled and deveined
¾ to 1 pound fresh or frozen skinless white-fleshed fish fillets, such as cod, haddock, or whiting, thawed if frozen, cut into 2-inch pieces
½ cup dry white wine
1 bag (12 ounces) frozen okra

2 large tomatoes, chopped
1 medium-sized onion, chopped
1 large garlic clove, chopped
2 teaspoons seafood seasoning
1 pound fresh mussels, cleaned (see Note, page 192)
2 cans (6½ ounces each) chopped clams, undrained

In a large pot, combine the shrimp, fish, wine, okra, tomatoes, onion, garlic, and seafood seasoning over medium-high heat; bring to a boil, then reduce the heat to medium and cook for 4 to 5 minutes. Add the mussels and the chopped clams with their juice. Cover and cook for about 4 more minutes, or just until the mussels open; do not overcook. **Discard any mussels that do not open by themselves.**

Clam and Linguine Special

4 to 6 servings

Ethel and I have spent many summers in beautiful Narragansett, Rhode Island, where there's a little clam shack on the beach that we love. Their linguine in clam sauce is worth a trip from anywhere! Okay, so if you're not up to a trip right now, you can bring home the same taste . . . but lighter.

1 pound uncooked linguine
1 medium-sized onion, chopped
4 ounces fresh mushrooms, sliced
   (about 2 cups)
2 teaspoons minced garlic
3 cans (6½ ounces each)
   chopped clams, undrained

1 tablespoon dried parsley flakes
½ teaspoon crushed red pepper
½ teaspoon dried oregano
1 bottle (8 ounces) clam juice,
   divided
2 tablespoons cornstarch

Cook the linguine according to the package directions; drain, rinse, drain again, and cover to keep warm. Meanwhile, place the onions, mushrooms, and garlic in a large skillet that has been coated with nonstick vegetable spray; cook over medium-high heat for 4 to 5 minutes, or until the onions and mushrooms are tender. Add the clams with their liquid, the parsley, red pepper, and oregano; stir in half the clam juice and bring to a boil. In a small bowl, combine the cornstarch with the remaining clam juice and stir until smooth; add to the skillet. Stir for 3 to 4 minutes, or until thickened. Toss with the warm linguine and serve immediately.

Linguine with Mussels

4 to 6 servings

Does eating pasta give you muscles? Well, this time it sure gives you mussels!

1 pound uncooked linguine
1 can (28 ounces) crushed
   tomatoes, undrained
1 pound fresh mussels, cleaned
   (see Note)
1 tablespoon dried parsley flakes

1 teaspoon dried oregano
1 teaspoon dried basil
½ teaspoon crushed red pepper
¼ teaspoon salt
¼ teaspoon black pepper

Cook the linguine according to the package directions. Drain, rinse, drain again; place in a large serving bowl and cover to keep warm. Meanwhile, in a large saucepan, heat the crushed tomatoes over medium heat until simmering. Add the mussels and cook for 2 minutes. Stir in the remaining ingredients. Cover and simmer over low heat for 3 to 5 minutes, until the mussels open. **Discard any mussels that do not open.** Pour over the hot pasta and toss until evenly combined. Serve immediately.

NOTE: Some fish markets sell mussels already cleaned and ready for cooking. If you buy mussels that aren't prepared, here's what to do: Wash them under cold running water and scrub away any grit or barnacles with a stiff food scrub brush. Remove the black "beard" from each mussel by cutting or pulling it off.

   If you'd like, top the finished dish with a couple tablespoons of grated Parmesan cheese after tossing to really bring out the Italian flavors.

Mussels Marinara

6 to 8 servings

If watching how *you* eat means *I* get to eat dishes like this one. . . .
Hooray for us all!

2 pounds fresh mussels, cleaned
   (see Note, page 192)
¼ cup dry white wine
1 can (14½ ounces) stewed
   tomatoes, chopped

½ teaspoon dried oregano
1 teaspoon salt
¼ teaspoon black pepper

Combine all the ingredients in a soup pot. Cover and bring to a
boil over high heat; reduce the heat to low and simmer for 6 to 8
minutes, or until the mussels open. Do not overcook. **Discard any
mussels that do not open.** Remove to a serving platter or individual
serving bowls and serve.

NOTE: Mussels are found in the seafood department of the supermarket, as well as in fish and seafood stores. They're reasonably
priced, so if you haven't given them a try, this is the time to go for
it. I think you'll be happy you did.

Salmon Burgers

6 sandwiches

Salmon burgers make fun sandwiches. Get the kids to help and have them form different-shaped burgers—some round, some square or triangular, or even oval-shaped ones that'll fit in hot dog buns.

1¾ cups dry bread crumbs, divided
1 can (15½ ounces) red salmon, drained and large bones discarded
1 can (10¾ ounces) reduced-fat condensed cream of mushroom soup

2 egg whites
1 teaspoon onion powder
1 teaspoon dried dillweed
¼ cup sweet pickle relish
Nonstick vegetable spray
6 sandwich buns, split and toasted

Preheat the broiler. Place ½ cup bread crumbs in a shallow dish; set aside. In a medium-sized bowl, combine all the remaining ingredients except the vegetable spray and buns; mix well. Form the mixture into 6 equal-sized ½-inch-thick patties. Coat the patties completely with the reserved bread crumbs and place on a rimmed baking sheet that has been coated with nonstick vegetable spray. Spray the patties lightly with nonstick vegetable spray and broil for 8 to 12 minutes, or until browned, turning halfway through the cooking. Serve on the buns.

NOTE: Add lettuce and tomato along with your favorite condiments to make really super sandwiches. You can also have these as great appetizers by making bite-sized patties and reducing the cooking time by a few minutes. I like to use red salmon because it gives the burgers nice color. Sure, the less-expensive pink salmon will work here, too.

Tuna in the Boat

4 to 6 servings

Here's one that won't get away! It even survives reheating in the oven or the microwave. Oh, it's especially good with a bowl of soup on rainy days.

8 ounces uncooked pasta shells
1 can (10¾ ounces) reduced-fat
   condensed cream of
   mushroom soup
1½ cups low-fat milk
1 package (10 ounces) frozen peas
   and carrots, thawed and
   drained

1 can (6 ounces) water-packed
   tuna, drained and flaked
½ teaspoon salt
¼ teaspoon black pepper
⅓ cup cornflake crumbs

Preheat the oven to 350°F. Cook the pasta according to the package directions; drain, rinse, drain again, and place in a large bowl. In a small bowl, combine the soup and milk; add to the pasta along with the remaining ingredients except the cornflake crumbs. Spoon into a 2-quart casserole dish that has been coated with nonstick vegetable spray. Sprinkle with the cornflake crumbs and bake for 35 to 40 minutes, or until browned on top and heated through.

NOTE: Have the kids make a ship's "mast" of fresh-cut veggies. Then watch how they sail through lunch or dinner!

MEATLESS MAIN DISHES

Meatless Main Dishes

Have you ever been at a dinner with someone who had requested a special meatless meal and the person was presented with a big plate of plain steamed vegetables as a main course? When people think of meatless meals, they think of boring dishes that lack variety and taste. Well, I'm about to change that! Let's start by thinking of all the meatless dishes we eat regularly . . . simply because we like them! There's meatless lasagna, pizza, pasta, soup. . . . Come on, flip the page and check them all out. I'm not saying that you have to forget about meat entirely, but, mixed into your diet, meatless meals are a nice light change of pace.

- Feature entrées with beans, pasta, and rice.
- Toss pasta with vegetables and some warm vegetable broth and seasonings for a quick dinner.
- Remember the five-a-day rule about eating at least five servings a day of fruit and vegetables. That's sure a good way to get our recommended allowances. And if you're trying to eat less meat and poultry, eating more fruit and vegetables means you'll eat less of those.
- Pizza is a great meatless main course option. And by simply topping a prepared pizza shell with tomato sauce, drained canned beans, and vegetables, you create a filling and nutritious entrée.
- Move your baked potato from the side to the center of the plate and top it with a low-fat topping like salsa or cooked vegetables or a prepared low-fat sauce to turn it into a colorful, crunchy, exciting main course.

Meatless Main Dishes

Carefree Vegetable Chili

6 to 8 servings

Never had chili without meat? Don't worry . . . neither you nor your family will miss the meat. In fact, it tastes so good that nobody'll even care. (That's how it got its name!)

1 tablespoon olive oil
1 large onion, chopped
1 can (28 ounces) crushed
    tomatoes, undrained
⅔ cup picante sauce
1½ teaspoons chili powder
1½ teaspoons ground cumin
¾ teaspoon salt

2 cans (15 to 16 ounces each) red
    kidney beans, rinsed and
    drained
1 large red bell pepper, chopped
1 large zucchini, cut into ½-inch
    chunks
1 medium-sized yellow squash,
    cut into ½-inch chunks

In a large saucepan, heat the oil over medium heat. Sauté the onion for 2 to 3 minutes. Add the tomatoes, picante sauce, chili powder, cumin, and salt. Reduce the heat to low, cover, and simmer for 10 minutes. Add the remaining ingredients, cover, and simmer for 10 minutes.

NOTE: For a change of flavor, I often like to use black beans instead of red kidney beans, so go ahead and use your favorite.

Spaghetti Squash Alfredo

4 to 6 servings

I think that too many people pass right by the spaghetti squash in the supermarket produce section simply because they don't know what it is or how to prepare it. Well, not only is it a fun dish to serve, but it's a fresh-tasting, low-fat, low-calorie option for combining with flavorful toppings. C'mon, give spaghetti squash a chance!

1 medium-sized spaghetti squash	¼ cup grated Parmesan cheese
1 cup reduced-fat sour cream	¼ teaspoon garlic powder
½ cup (2 ounces) shredded part-	¼ teaspoon salt
skim mozzarella cheese	¼ teaspoon black pepper

Fill a soup pot with 1 inch of water and place the whole squash in the water. Bring to a boil over medium-high heat, cover, and cook for 25 to 30 minutes, or until tender when pierced with a knife. Remove it to a cutting board and allow to cool slightly, about 15 minutes. In a medium-sized saucepan, combine the remaining ingredients over medium-low heat and whisk until smooth and creamy, stirring frequently to prevent burning. Cut the squash in half lengthwise, then use a soup spoon to remove and discard the seeds. Scrape the inside of the squash with a fork, shredding it into noodle-like strands. Add the strands to the sauce and stir until thoroughly mixed and heated through. Serve immediately.

NOTE: If you want to save some time, cut the raw squash in half lengthwise and place in a microwave-safe covered casserole dish with 2 tablespoons water; microwave for 10 to 12 minutes, or until tender. Be careful when cutting raw spaghetti squash. The outer skin is very hard.

Fresh Veggie Burgers

6 patties

Veggie burgers have become "the rage." And, why not: They're hearty, tasty, and often cholesterol- and fat-free. Here's a version you can make at home. Sure, it's a little more work than simply thawing frozen patties, but wait till you taste the difference!

¾ cup dry bread crumbs, divided
1 tablespoon canola or
    vegetable oil
1 medium-sized onion, finely
    chopped
2 garlic cloves, minced
1 teaspoon dried thyme
3 cups cooked brown rice,
    warmed

1 medium-sized carrot, peeled and
    grated
⅓ cup chopped fresh parsley
¼ cup grated Parmesan cheese
3 tablespoons light soy sauce
½ cup egg substitute

Preheat the broiler. Place ½ cup bread crumbs in a shallow dish and set aside. In a large nonstick skillet, heat the oil over medium-high heat. Sauté the onion, garlic, and thyme for 4 to 5 minutes, or until the onion is tender. Place in a large bowl and add the remaining ingredients (except the reserved bread crumbs); mix well. Form the mixture into six ½-inch-thick patties and coat with the reserved ½ cup bread crumbs. Place on a rimmed baking sheet that has been coated with nonstick vegetable spray. Broil for 12 to 14 minutes, or until golden and heated through, turning halfway through the broiling.

NOTE: Serve on a bun with lettuce and tomato for an unbeatable sandwich. Oh—your favorite type of brown rice, even a quick-cooking one, will work great in this recipe.

Italian Spaghetti Squash

4 to 6 servings

Why not let your garden (or supermarket produce department!) supply your main dish? It can be so abundant—or, as they say in Italy, *abbondante!*

1 medium-sized spaghetti squash
2 medium-sized zucchini, sliced
    into ¼-inch rounds
1 medium-sized onion, chopped
1 cup sliced fresh mushrooms

¼ teaspoon garlic powder
½ teaspoon salt
¼ teaspoon black pepper
1 jar (16 ounces) light spaghetti
    sauce

Fill a soup pot with 1 inch of water and place the whole squash in the water. Bring to a boil over medium-high heat, cover, and cook for 25 to 30 minutes, or until tender when pierced with a knife. (See note on page 204.) Meanwhile, in a medium-sized saucepan that has been coated with nonstick vegetable spray, cook the zucchini, onion, mushrooms, garlic powder, salt, and pepper over medium-low heat for 8 to 10 minutes, or until the vegetables are tender. Add the spaghetti sauce and stir to blend; continue cooking until warmed through. When the squash is tender, remove it to a cutting board and allow to cool slightly, about 15 minutes. Cut the squash in half lengthwise, then use a soup spoon to remove and discard the seeds. Scrape the inside of the squash with a fork, shredding it into noodle-like strands. Add the strands to the sauce and stir until thoroughly mixed and heated through. Serve immediately.

Corn-Stuffed Squash

4 servings

It's fancy enough for a holiday dinner, but easy enough for a week-day family meal.

2 acorn squash (about 4 pounds)
2 cans (11 ounces each)
    Mexican-style corn, drained
2 egg whites

½ cup dry bread crumbs, divided
½ teaspoon salt
¼ teaspoon black pepper
Nonstick vegetable spray

Preheat the oven to 350°F. Cut each acorn squash in half length-wise; remove the seeds and place cut side down in a 9" × 13" baking dish that has been coated with nonstick vegetable spray. Bake for 50 to 60 minutes, or until tender. Meanwhile, in a small bowl, combine the corn, egg whites, all but 2 tablespoons of the bread crumbs, the salt, and pepper. Remove the squash from the oven and carefully turn them over. Place ¼ of the bread crumb mixture in each squash half. Sprinkle evenly with the remaining 2 table-spoons bread crumbs, then spray with nonstick vegetable spray. Return to the oven and bake for 25 to 30 minutes, or until the filling is set and the tops are golden.

NOTE: You can serve this as a side dish or a main dish. For a main dish, ½ squash should equal 1 serving. For a side dish, ½ squash should be 2 servings, so you can cut each half of the cooked squash in half.

Bow Tie Vegetable Salad

4 to 6 servings

Don't you just love all the different shapes of pasta that we can get these days? Here's one that helps us "dress up" a meal.

8 ounces uncooked bow tie pasta
8 ounces fresh mushrooms, sliced (about 3 cups)
1 large red bell pepper, cut into 1-inch chunks
2 cans (14 ounces each) artichoke hearts, drained and cut in half
1 medium-sized tomato, cut into 8 wedges
1 cup light or other spaghetti sauce
½ teaspoon ground cumin
1 teaspoon salt
¼ teaspoon black pepper
2 tablespoons grated Parmesan cheese

Prepare the pasta according to the package directions; drain, rinse, and drain again. Place in a large bowl, set aside and cover to keep warm. Meanwhile, coat a large nonstick skillet with nonstick vegetable spray. Add the mushrooms, bell pepper, and artichokes and sauté over medium-high heat for 6 to 8 minutes, or until tender and no liquid remains. Stir in the tomato, sauce, cumin, salt, and black pepper and continue cooking until thoroughly heated. Add the vegetable mixture to the pasta and toss to mix. Sprinkle with the Parmesan cheese and serve immediately.

Penne and Parsley Pesto

4 to 6 servings

Traditional pesto sauce is made with fresh basil, but I've lightened up the taste of this one by using fresh parsley. And I've lightened up the fat by using low-fat yogurt instead of all oil.

1 pound uncooked penne pasta
3 cups firmly packed fresh parsley
    leaves
½ cup plain low-fat yogurt
⅓ cup chopped walnuts
¼ cup grated Parmesan cheese

2 tablespoons olive oil
1 teaspoon garlic powder
½ teaspoon salt
¾ cup ready-to-use chicken broth
½ cup chopped roasted red
    peppers

Cook the pasta according to the package directions; drain, rinse, and drain again. Return the pasta to its cooking pot. Meanwhile, in a blender or a food processor that has been fitted with its steel cutting blade, combine the parsley, yogurt, walnuts, Parmesan cheese, oil, garlic powder, and salt. Blend until thoroughly mixed; pour over the pasta. Add the chicken broth and roasted peppers; mix well and warm over medium heat for 2 to 3 minutes, or until thoroughly heated.

Spinach and Cheese Manicotti

4 to 6 servings

If up till now you've shied away from making manicotti 'cause you thought it was hard to do, it's time to think again!

8 ounces uncooked manicotti
  shells
Nonstick vegetable spray
1 container (32 ounces) part-
  skim ricotta cheese
2 cups (8 ounces) shredded part-
  skim mozzarella cheese
½ cup grated Parmesan cheese,
  divided

¼ cup egg substitute
¼ teaspoon salt
¼ teaspoon black pepper
1 package (10 ounces) frozen
  chopped spinach, thawed and
  squeezed dry
1 jar (16 ounces) light spaghetti
  sauce

Preheat the oven to 350°F. Prepare the manicotti shells according to the package directions; drain, rinse, and drain again. Spray the pasta lightly with nonstick vegetable spray. In a large bowl, combine the ricotta cheese, mozzarella cheese, ¼ cup Parmesan cheese, the egg substitute, salt, and pepper. Add the spinach and mix well. Fill each manicotti shell with about ⅓ cup of the cheese mixture (see Note), then place them in a 9" × 13" glass baking dish that has been coated with nonstick vegetable spray. Pour the spaghetti sauce over the shells and sprinkle with the remaining ¼ cup Parmesan cheese. Bake for 35 to 40 minutes, or until hot and bubbling.

NOTE: For an easy way to fill the manicotti shells, place the cheese mixture in a resealable plastic storage bag. Snip off a corner of the bag and squeeze the cheese mixture into the shells. Oh—for an extra burst of flavor, add ⅛ teaspoon ground nutmeg to the ricotta cheese mixture.

RESEALABLE BAG

CHEESE MIX

SNIP THE CORNER

SQUEEZE MIXTURE INTO MANICOTTI SHELL

Spicy Baked Linguine

6 to 8 servings

If there was an Olympic competition for pasta, this one would definitely take the gold!

1 pound uncooked linguine
1 tablespoon sunflower or
    vegetable oil
1 medium-sized zucchini, cut into
    1-inch chunks
1 large red bell pepper, cut into
    1-inch chunks
1 jar (26 ounces) light spaghetti
    sauce
1 cup salsa
¾ cup (3 ounces) shredded
    reduced-fat mozzarella cheese

Preheat the oven to 350°F. Cook the linguine according to the package directions; drain, rinse, drain again, and set aside. Meanwhile, heat the oil in a soup pot over medium-high heat; add the zucchini and bell pepper. Sauté for 6 to 8 minutes, or until tender. Stir in the spaghetti sauce and salsa, then add the linguine and mix well. Place the linguine mixture in a 9" × 13" baking dish that has been coated with nonstick vegetable spray. Top with the mozzarella cheese and bake for 25 to 30 minutes, or until the cheese is melted.

Spring-"thyme" Pasta

6 to 8 servings

This is good in springtime or anytime . . . 'cause to prepare it takes *no* time!

12 ounces uncooked tricolored rotelle or other twist pasta

3 cups broccoli florets

8 ounces fresh mushrooms, quartered (about 3 cups)

1 large red onion, cut in half and sliced

1 medium-sized red bell pepper, cut into ¼-inch strips

1 can (10½ ounces) condensed chicken broth

2 teaspoons dried basil

1 teaspoon dried thyme

¼ teaspoon crushed red pepper

½ teaspoon salt

1 container (16 ounces) reduced-fat sour cream

Cook the pasta according to the package directions; drain, rinse, drain again, and set aside in a large bowl. Cover to keep warm. Meanwhile, coat a large nonstick skillet with nonstick vegetable spray. Add the broccoli, mushrooms, onion, and bell pepper; cook over medium-high heat for 2 to 3 minutes, stirring often. Add the broth, basil, thyme, crushed red pepper, and salt; mix until well combined. Bring to a boil and cook for 2 to 3 minutes, stirring occasionally. Reduce the heat to low, then stir in the sour cream and stir until heated through. Pour over the pasta; toss and serve immediately.

Penne Italiano

6 to 8 servings

Before dinner, ask your gang if they'll give you a penny for your thoughts. Then ask if *you* can give *them* some penne for dinner! Think they'll get it? (I know they'll eat it up!)

8 ounces uncooked penne pasta
1 head salad savoy or escarole, shredded
4 cups water
2 chicken bouillon cubes

¼ teaspoon crushed red pepper
⅛ teaspoon black pepper
3 cans (16 ounces each) Great Northern beans, rinsed and drained

Prepare the pasta according to the package directions; drain, rinse, and drain again. Set aside. In a soup pot, combine the salad savoy, water, bouillon cubes, crushed red pepper, and black pepper over medium heat. Simmer for 30 to 35 minutes, or until the salad savoy is tender. Add the beans and cook for 10 minutes, or until thoroughly heated and slightly thickened. Stir in the pasta and cook until heated through; serve immediately.

NOTE: I like to add ½ teaspoon salt to really bring out the great flavors.

New-Twist Macaroni and Cheese

6 to 8 servings

I've got a '50s comfort food mixed with a today twist. What's the twist? I'll give you a hint . . . it's the salsa!

1 pound uncooked elbow
    macaroni
1 container (16 ounces) reduced-
    fat sour cream
2 egg whites
½ cup mild salsa
½ cup low-fat milk

¾ teaspoon dry mustard
1 teaspoon salt
¾ teaspoon black pepper
2 cups (8 ounces) shredded
    reduced-fat Cheddar cheese
¼ cup grated Parmesan cheese

Preheat the oven to 350°F. Prepare the macaroni according to the package directions. Drain, rinse, and drain again; set aside. In a large bowl, combine the sour cream, egg whites, salsa, milk, mustard, salt, and pepper; mix well. Add the Cheddar cheese and mix well. Add the macaroni and toss until well mixed. Pour into a 2-quart casserole dish that has been coated with nonstick vegetable spray. Sprinkle evenly with the Parmesan cheese and bake for 30 to 40 minutes, or until lightly browned.

NOTE: For a little added color, sprinkle on ½ teaspoon dried parsley flakes along with the Parmesan.

Bottomless Vegetable Lasagna

6 to 9 servings

Why "bottomless"? Because there are no noodles on the bottom as in regular lasagna. And once you taste it, you're gonna wish it was in a bottomless *pan*!

1 can (10¾ ounces) reduced-fat
    condensed cream of
    chicken soup
1 container (15 ounces) part-
    skim ricotta cheese
4 ounces reduced-fat cream
    cheese, softened
1 package (16 ounces) frozen
    broccoli, carrots, and
    cauliflower, thawed

1 package (10 ounces) frozen
    peas, thawed
6 uncooked lasagna noodles
1 cup (4 ounces) shredded
    reduced-fat mozzarella cheese,
    divided

Preheat the oven to 350°F. Coat a 9" × 13" glass baking dish with nonstick vegetable spray. In a large bowl, combine the soup, ricotta cheese and cream cheese; add the frozen vegetables and mix well. Spread ⅓ of the vegetable mixture in the bottom of the baking dish. Press 3 lasagna noodles into the vegetable mixture. Spread ½ of the remaining vegetable mixture over the noodles. Sprinkle with ½ cup mozzarella cheese. Arrange 3 noodles on top, pressing down gently; top with the remaining vegetable mixture. Cover tightly with aluminum foil and bake for 1 hour and 20 minutes. Remove the foil and sprinkle with the remaining ½ cup mozzarella cheese. Return to the oven and bake for 5 more minutes, or until the cheese is golden and melted.

Family Gnocchi

4 to 5 servings

Wait till your family tries your fresh homemade pasta . . . and you don't even need a pasta machine for this one!

2 pounds potatoes, peeled and quartered
1 cup egg substitute

3 to 3½ cups all-purpose flour, divided
2 teaspoons salt
½ teaspoon black pepper

Place the potatoes in a large saucepan and add just enough water to cover them. Bring to a boil over high heat, then reduce the heat to medium and cook for 20 to 25 minutes, or until the potatoes are fork-tender. Drain the potatoes and allow to cool to room temperature. Meanwhile, bring another large pot of water to boil over high heat. Place the cooled potatoes in a medium-sized bowl and mash with a fork. Add the egg substitute, 3 cups flour, the salt, and pepper; mix well. If necessary, add additional flour, 1 teaspoon at a time, until the mixture is firm enough to handle (and not sticky). Pinch off ½-inch pieces from the dough and place on a waxed paper–covered baking sheet. Carefully drop into the boiling water. Cook for 4 to 5 minutes, or until the gnocchi rise to the top and the centers are cooked, stirring occasionally; drain and serve.

NOTE: Warm up some of your favorite prepared or home-made tomato sauce for serving with these.

Tex-Mex Potatoes

4 servings

Baked potatoes have always been a popular standard. And now that Tex-Mex food has become so popular everywhere, why not enjoy that bang-up flavor in a potato side dish or main course.

4 large baking potatoes, scrubbed and pierced with a fork
1 cup low-fat cottage cheese
¼ teaspoon salt
¼ teaspoon black pepper

½ cup (2 ounces) shredded reduced-fat Cheddar cheese
½ cup mild salsa
1 scallion, chopped

Preheat the oven to 400°F. Place the potatoes on a rimmed baking sheet and bake for 1 to 1½ hours, or until fork-tender. In a small bowl, combine the cottage cheese, salt, and pepper. Remove the potatoes from the oven and cut a slit in the top of each. Squeeze the ends together, forming pockets. Spoon ¼ cup of the cottage cheese mixture into each potato. Sprinkle evenly with the Cheddar cheese and top with the salsa and chopped scallion. Serve immediately.

NOTE: For faster baked potatoes, you could "bake" them in your microwave, according to the manufacturer's directions.

Hakuna Frittata

4 servings

After I made this frittata, my granddaughter sang me a song about it. Well, that's what she *thought* were the words of her favorite song. What I wanted to do for you with this recipe is give you no worries . . . and I hope that you agree!

2 medium-sized baking potatoes
1 cup chopped fresh mushrooms
½ cup chopped broccoli florets
2 scallions, chopped
⅓ cup chopped red bell pepper
1 garlic clove, crushed

⅛ teaspoon crushed red pepper
½ teaspoon salt
3 whole eggs
3 egg whites
¼ cup low-fat milk

Bake the potatoes in a preheated 400°F. oven for about 1 hour, or in the microwave oven on high power for 7 to 10 minutes, until just tender. Let cool slightly, then cut into ½-inch chunks. Coat a large nonstick skillet with nonstick vegetable spray and heat over medium-high heat. Add the potatoes, mushrooms, broccoli, scallions, bell pepper, garlic, crushed red pepper, and salt. Cook for 2 to 3 minutes, stirring occasionally, or until the vegetables are tender and the potatoes are lightly browned. While the vegetables are cooking, in a medium-sized bowl, whisk together the eggs, egg whites, and milk. Reduce the skillet heat to medium-low and add the egg mixture. As the mixture begins to set, push the cooked edges slightly toward the center, allowing the liquid to run out to the edges of the skillet. Reduce the heat to low and cover the skillet. Allow to cook for 8 to 9 minutes, or until the eggs are set. Slide the frittata out of the pan onto a serving plate. Cut into 4 wedges and serve immediately.

Taco 'Tatoes

4 servings

We all love tacos, and we all love baked potatoes. It's only natural to combine these two favorites to get a dish worthy of a grand "Olé!"

4 large baking potatoes, scrubbed and pierced with a fork
1 medium-sized onion, chopped
1 can (15 to 16 ounces) red kidney beans, undrained

1 tablespoon taco seasoning
1 cup shredded lettuce
1 medium-sized tomato, chopped
½ cup reduced-fat sour cream

Preheat the oven to 400°F. Place the potatoes on a rimmed baking sheet and bake for 1 to 1½ hours, or until fork-tender. Meanwhile, in a large nonstick skillet that has been coated with nonstick vegetable spray, cook the onion over medium-high heat for 5 to 6 minutes, or until tender and lightly browned. Add the beans and taco seasoning; mix well and continue cooking for 2 to 3 minutes, or until heated through. Remove the potatoes from the oven and cut a slit in the top of each. Squeeze the ends together, forming pockets. Place each potato on a plate and top with the bean mixture, lettuce, tomatoes, and sour cream. Serve immediately.

NOTE: For faster baked potatoes, you could "bake" them in your microwave, according to the manufacturer's directions.

Spanish Rice and Beans

6 to 8 servings

When I was a kid, Mom's Spanish rice was one of our favorite main courses. It was loaded with beef. Okay, in this version I wanted to keep that great taste but cut back on the fat. By replacing the beef with black beans, I was able to do just that. Mom would be proud!

2 cups long- or whole-grain rice
1 can (14½ ounces) stewed
    tomatoes, undrained
2¼ cups water
1 cup salsa
2 tablespoons Worcestershire
    sauce

1½ teaspoons sugar
1 teaspoon hot pepper sauce
1 teaspoon salt
1 can (16 ounces) black beans,
    rinsed and drained

In a soup pot, combine all the ingredients except the beans over medium-high heat and bring to a boil. Reduce the heat to low, cover, and simmer for 30 minutes. Stir in the beans and remove from the heat. Allow to sit, covered, for 20 to 25 minutes, or until the liquid is absorbed and the rice is tender.

NOTE: You can substitute your favorite kind of canned beans for the black beans, if you prefer.

Quick Baked Falafel

5 to 6 servings

This is a baked version of the popular Middle Eastern dish that is typically panfried in lots of oil. It's high in protein . . . and the taste is the tops!

1 can (15 to 19 ounces) garbanzo beans (chick peas), rinsed and drained
1 cup dry bread crumbs
2 egg whites
2 tablespoons chopped fresh parsley

2 teaspoons lemon juice
1 teaspoon garlic powder
½ teaspoon ground cumin
½ teaspoon salt
½ teaspoon black pepper
Nonstick vegetable spray

Preheat the oven to 400°F. Place all the ingredients except the vegetable spray in a food processor that has been fitted with its steel cutting blade. Process until well blended. Shape the mixture into 1½-inch balls and place 2 inches apart on a 10" × 15" rimmed baking sheet that has been coated with nonstick vegetable spray. With the palm of your hand, flatten the balls into ½-inch-thick patties. Spray the tops with nonstick vegetable spray. Bake for 20 minutes, or until golden brown on both sides, turning halfway through the cooking.

NOTE: One serving is 3 or 4 patties in a warm pita bread with chopped lettuce and tomatoes.

DISHES

Side Dishes

Side dishes are like the supporting cast in a show or movie. Their job is to make the main dish (or star) shine! The side dish should supplement without taking anything away from the star of the meal. And when you start cooking a little lighter, it's just as important to make sure the side dishes are lighter, too. With a few tips, you'll be on your way to making supporting side dishes worthy of the top awards!

- If using prepared mayonnaise, dressings, or dairy products, try using reduced-fat versions, as well as cutting down on the amounts used.
- Don't smother vegetables, potatoes, rice, or beans with a load of butter. Use it sparingly, to keep the rich taste but still cut down on the fat. Experiment with your spice rack, too!
- Instead of boiling vegetables, steam or grill them—and keep them a bit crunchy so as to enjoy their natural taste and get more nutritional value from them. Besides, overcooking them robs them of their bright color and fresh texture.
- It's not necessary to add salt and oil to the cooking water when boiling pasta!
- Try using no-yolk noodles in place of traditional egg noodles. They're available right in your supermarket pasta section.
- Instead of frying potatoes in oil, spray them lightly with nonstick vegetable spray and bake them.

- Brown, basmati, and other rices offer a nice change from tra-ditional white rice. They have different tastes, so keep mealtime exciting by trying a variety. (They often take longer to cook than white rice, so check for doneness.)
- Warm honey or jelly makes a nice glaze for steamed fresh or frozen vegetables (without adding much fat or cholesterol).

Side Dishes

DISHES

Garlic-Baked "Smashed" Potatoes

4 to 6 servings

Smashing! I mean what you do to these *and* how they taste. Now, because they're baked, there's no water to boil. So they're not only garlic-delicious, they're easy, too!

10 medium-sized red-skinned
   potatoes (about 3 pounds),
   washed and pierced with
   a fork
1 small onion, unpeeled, cut in
   half crosswise

8 to 10 garlic cloves, peeled
1½ cups low-fat milk
1 teaspoon salt
¼ teaspoon black pepper

Preheat the oven to 425°F. Place the potatoes and the onion cut sides down on a large rimmed baking sheet that has been coated with nonstick vegetable spray and bake for 40 minutes. Add the garlic to the baking sheet and bake for 10 to 15 minutes, until the potatoes and garlic are tender. Remove from the oven and allow to cool slightly. Meanwhile, in a small saucepan, combine the milk, salt, and pepper and heat over low heat for 3 to 4 minutes; do not boil. Cut the potatoes into quarters and peel the onion. Place the potatoes, onion, and garlic in a large bowl and "smash" with a potato masher or a fork. Add the milk mixture and continue to "smash" to mix well. Serve.

NOTE: I don't mind lumpy mashed potatoes. I guess that's because my mother made them that way! But if you prefer a smoother version, just beat them with an electric beater instead of a potato masher.

Baked Stuffed Potatoes

6 servings

Here's a way to supervise how much butter and sour cream your family gets with their potatoes. It's not a problem, because you bake 'em, mix 'em, and stuff 'em. So there's no need to serve additional toppings!

6 medium-sized baking potatoes,
    scrubbed and pierced with
    a fork
¼ cup reduced-fat sour cream
1 tablespoon butter
¼ teaspoon onion powder

½ teaspoon salt
¼ teaspoon black pepper
Paprika for sprinkling

Preheat the oven to 400°F. Place the potatoes on a rimmed baking sheet and bake for 1 to 1½ hours, or until fork-tender. Slice 1 inch lengthwise off the top of each potato and scoop out the pulp from the top and bottom pieces, placing all the pulp in a medium-sized bowl and discarding the potato tops. Add the sour cream, butter, onion powder, salt, and pepper; using an electric beater on medium speed, mix until smooth and creamy. Spoon the mixture back into the potato shells and place on the baking sheet. Sprinkle lightly with paprika and bake for 20 to 30 minutes, or until the tops of the potatoes begin to brown.

Party Potatoes

4 to 6 servings

Entertaining is a snap when you've got easy and tasty dishes to serve. And the combination of spices in these roasted potatoes has just enough bite to make them the talk of the party!

2 teaspoons paprika
1 teaspoon garlic powder
1 teaspoon onion powder
2 teaspoons salt
½ teaspoon black pepper

8 medium-sized red-skinned
    potatoes (about 2½ pounds),
    washed and cut into 1-inch
    chunks
1 tablespoon vegetable oil
Nonstick vegetable spray

Preheat the oven to 400°F. In a small bowl, combine the paprika, garlic and onion powders, salt, and pepper; mix well. In a large bowl, toss the potatoes with the oil. Add the spice mixture and toss until the potatoes are well coated. Spread the potatoes in a single layer on a large rimmed baking sheet that has been coated with nonstick vegetable spray. Bake for 45 to 50 minutes, or until fork-tender, turning the potatoes occasionally and coating them with vegetable spray halfway through the baking.

Sweet Potato and Cherry Surprise

6 to 8 servings

I wasn't sure whether to put this in the side dish or dessert chapter, but since my family loved having it along with their dinner, here it is! It's a thumbs-up winner either way.

2 cans (29 ounces each) yams, drained
2 egg whites
¼ cup firmly packed light brown sugar
½ teaspoon ground cinnamon
1 can (21 ounces) cherry pie filling
Nonstick vegetable spray

Preheat the oven to 350°F. In a large bowl, combine the yams, egg whites, brown sugar, and cinnamon; mash until well mixed. Spoon half of the mixture into a 10-inch deep-dish pie pan that has been coated with nonstick vegetable spray, spreading it evenly over the bottom and up the sides of the pan to create a "crust." Pour the cherry pie filling into the "crust," then cover with the remaining yam mixture. Spray the top of the pie with vegetable spray and bake on the middle oven rack for 55 to 60 minutes, or until set and the top is golden. Allow to cool slightly before serving.

Baked Sweet Potato Fries

3 to 4 servings

Are these a new type of French fry? Why not?! You can eat them with a burger or all by themselves. They've got a friendly bite no matter what you serve them with.

1 tablespoon chili powder
1 teaspoon salt
¼ teaspoon black pepper

6 large sweet potatoes, peeled and cut lengthwise into thin wedges
Nonstick vegetable spray

Preheat the oven to 425°F. In a large resealable plastic storage bag, combine the chili powder, salt, and pepper. Add the potato wedges in batches and shake until completely coated. Spread the potato wedges in a single layer on rimmed baking sheets that have been coated with nonstick vegetable spray. Coat the potatoes with vegetable spray and bake for 22 to 25 minutes, or until golden and tender.

NOTE: To make these crispy, combine the seasonings with 2 beaten egg whites in a shallow dish. Coat the potato wedges with this mixture and bake as above.

Mom's Scalloped Potatoes

6 servings

These may be as good as Mom's (and they were great), but without all the fat. I mean, today we can enjoy Mom's great flavor combinations with a moderate approach.

1 can (10¾ ounces) reduced-fat
   condensed cream of
   mushroom soup
¾ cup low-fat milk
½ cup reduced-fat sour cream
1 teaspoon onion powder

1 teaspoon salt
¼ teaspoon white pepper
1 package (32 ounces) frozen
   shredded potatoes, thawed
⅛ teaspoon paprika
1 scallion, sliced

Preheat the oven to 400°F. In a large bowl, combine the soup, milk, sour cream, onion powder, salt, and pepper. Add the potatoes and toss until evenly coated. Place in a 2-quart casserole dish that has been coated with nonstick vegetable spray. Sprinkle with the paprika, cover, and bake for 25 minutes. Remove the cover and bake for 35 to 40 more minutes, or until golden on top. Sprinkle with the scallions and serve immediately.

Fast Mashed Potatoes and Parsnips

4 to 6 servings

If you're looking for a change from plain mashed potatoes, you've found it! The parsnips give a delightful earthy flavor to each forkful.

6 large potatoes, peeled and
    quartered
6 medium-sized parsnips, peeled
    and cut into 1-inch chunks
2 medium-sized onions, peeled
    and cut into 8 wedges each

4 garlic cloves, peeled
⅔ cup reduced-fat sour cream
1½ teaspoons salt
¼ teaspoon black pepper

Fill a large pot ¾-full with water; add the potatoes, parsnips, onions, and garlic. Cover and bring to a boil over medium-high heat; reduce the heat to medium-low and cook for 20 minutes, or until the vegetables are tender. Drain and transfer to a large bowl. Add the sour cream, salt, and pepper and beat with an electric beater for 3 to 4 minutes, or until creamy.

NOTE: You can make these a day or two before planning to serve them. Then you can just heat 'em in the microwave for a few minutes before mealtime.

Home-Style Mashed Potatoes

6 to 8 servings

Nothing says "home" like a big bowl of homemade mashed potatoes. If you've never made them from scratch, now's the time— especially since they don't have to be full of calories to be loaded with taste.

5 pounds potatoes, peeled and
    quartered
1 cup low-fat milk
2 ounces reduced-fat cream
    cheese, softened

¼ teaspoon onion powder
1 tablespoon salt
¼ teaspoon black pepper

Place the potatoes in a large pot and add just enough water to cover the potatoes. Bring to a boil over medium-high heat. Reduce the heat to medium-low; cover and cook for 20 minutes, or until the potatoes are fork-tender. Drain and place the potatoes in a large bowl. Add the remaining ingredients. Beat with an electric beater on medium speed for 3 to 4 minutes, or until the potatoes are light and fluffy. Serve immediately.

Cold Sesame Noodles

4 to 6 servings

I happen to be a peanut butter fan, but even if you're not, I think you'll find this dish very interesting . . . and (I hope) very delicious!

1 pound uncooked linguine or
    spaghetti
1 cup reduced-fat peanut butter
6 scallions, thinly sliced
2 tablespoons vegetable oil
2 tablespoons light soy sauce

1 tablespoon finely chopped
    garlic
1½ teaspoons white vinegar
1 teaspoon sesame oil
¼ teaspoon cayenne pepper

Prepare the pasta according to the package directions. Drain, rinse, drain again, and set aside. In a large bowl, combine the remaining ingredients; mix well. Add the pasta and toss to coat evenly. Cover and chill for at least 1 hour before serving.

NOTE: Sure, you can serve this warm, but to really bring out the sesame and peanut flavors, I prefer it cold.

Spaghetti Rice

5 to 6 servings

I'll bet you never thought of serving spaghetti and rice in the same bowl, did you? I think you're gonna be pleasantly surprised at how well they go together . . . I was!

2 tablespoons vegetable oil, divided
1 can (4 ounces) sliced mushrooms, drained
1 medium-sized onion, chopped
1 cup (about 4 ounces) uncooked spaghetti broken into 3-inch pieces

1½ cups long- or whole-grain rice
2 cans (14½ ounces each) ready-to-use chicken broth
¼ teaspoon salt
⅛ teaspoon black pepper

In a large saucepan, heat 1 tablespoon oil over medium-high heat; add the mushrooms and onions and sauté until lightly browned. Remove from the pan and set aside. Heat the remaining 1 tablespoon oil and brown the spaghetti over medium-low heat. (Be careful—it browns quickly.) Remove the pan from the heat and add the mushrooms and onions, along with the remaining ingredients; mix well. Bring the mixture to a boil over medium-high heat; reduce the heat to low, cover, and cook for 20 more minutes, or until all the liquid is absorbed.

Anytime Fried Rice

4 to 6 servings

You don't have to be serving up a complete Chinese dinner to serve fried rice. And with no egg and minimal oil, this one's a 1-2-3 throw-together that's quick and ready to go in no time.

2 tablespoons vegetable oil
3 cups cold cooked white rice, rinsed
1 package (10 ounces) frozen peas, thawed

6 scallions, sliced
⅓ cup light soy sauce
¼ cup ready-to-use chicken broth
¼ teaspoon black pepper

In a large skillet, heat the oil over medium-high heat. Add the rice and stir-fry for 10 minutes; add the peas and scallions and continue to stir-fry for 1 minute. Add the remaining ingredients; mix well. Reduce the heat to medium-low and cook, stirring, for 2 to 3 minutes, or until thoroughly mixed and heated through.

NOTE: Using moist cold rice helps to give it that crisp fried rice texture and flavor. And for an extra dash of flavor, mix ¼ teaspoon garlic powder with the chicken broth.

Mushroom and Zucchini Risotto

6 to 8 servings

Whoa! I hope you won't pass this by simply because it uses Parmesan cheese. There's only half a cup in the whole dish—Parmesan is a high-flavored cheese that goes a long way.

2 medium-sized onions, chopped
8 ounces fresh mushrooms, sliced
2 teaspoons minced garlic
2 cups long- or whole-grain rice
1 medium-sized zucchini, coarsely shredded
1 can (14½ ounces) ready-to-use chicken broth

3 cups water
2 teaspoons dried Italian seasoning
½ teaspoon salt
¼ teaspoon black pepper
½ cup grated Parmesan cheese

In a large saucepan that has been coated with nonstick vegetable spray, sauté the onions, mushrooms, and garlic over medium-high heat for 5 to 7 minutes, or until the onions are tender. Add the rice and zucchini and cook for 3 to 5 more minutes, or until the rice begins to brown. Meanwhile, in a medium-sized saucepan, combine the chicken broth, water, Italian seasoning, salt, and pepper. Bring to a boil over medium-high heat. Add to the rice mixture, cover, and simmer over low heat for 15 minutes. Add the Parmesan cheese and stir for 1 to 2 minutes, until creamy and well combined and all the liquid is absorbed.

Mushroom Rice Pilaf

4 to 6 servings

Rice sure is a great side dish when we're watching what we eat. The challenge is to keep the taste exciting. Go on, break the side-dish boredom by adding this to your repertoire.

2 tablespoons sunflower or
  vegetable oil
1 small onion, chopped
2 cups sliced fresh mushrooms
  (about 5 ounces)
1 can (10½ ounces) condensed
  chicken broth

1 cup uncooked long- or whole-
  grain rice
¾ cup water
1 teaspoon garlic powder
¼ teaspoon black pepper

In a large skillet, heat the oil over medium heat. Sauté the onion for 2 to 3 minutes, or until tender. Add the mushrooms and sauté for 3 to 4 more minutes, or until tender. Add the remaining ingredients; mix well. Bring to a boil, then reduce the heat to low. Cover and simmer for 25 to 30 minutes, or until no liquid remains. Serve immediately.

Nutty Brown Rice

5 to 6 servings

No nuts here . . . it just tastes like it 'cause brown rice gives us natural nutty flavor plus lots of vitamins. Of course, I make it because it tastes so good.

1 tablespoon sunflower or
    vegetable oil
1 small onion, chopped
1 can (10½ ounces) condensed
    chicken broth
¾ cup water
1 cup uncooked brown rice (not
    instant rice)

1 teaspoon ground cumin
½ teaspoon black pepper
1 can (16 ounces) Great
    Northern beans, rinsed and
    drained
4 plum tomatoes, chopped, seeds
    and juices squeezed out

In a large skillet, heat the oil over medium heat; add the onion and sauté for 2 to 3 minutes, or until tender. Add the broth, water, rice, cumin, and pepper; mix well. Bring to a boil, then reduce the heat to low. Cover and simmer for 30 minutes, or until all the liquid is absorbed. With a spoon, gently stir in the beans and tomatoes; cook for 5 minutes, or until heated through.

Mixed-up Roasted Vegetables

8 to 10 servings

Fancy restaurants serve these as an appetizer. Fairs serve these with sausage on a bun. Roasted vegetables fit any occasion, so what are you waiting for?!

4 medium-sized yellow squash, cut into ½-inch slices
3 medium-sized zucchini, cut into ½-inch slices
3 medium-sized onions, quartered
2 medium-sized green bell peppers, cut into 1½-inch chunks

1 medium-sized yellow bell pepper, cut into 1½-inch chunks
1 medium-sized red bell pepper, cut into 1½-inch chunks
2 tablespoons vegetable oil
1 teaspoon garlic powder
1 teaspoon salt
½ teaspoon black pepper

Preheat the oven to 450°F. Combine all the vegetables in a large bowl; toss. In a small bowl, combine the remaining ingredients; mix well. Drizzle over the vegetables and toss until well coated. Lay the vegetables in a single layer on 2 large rimmed baking sheets that have been coated with nonstick vegetable spray. Roast for 20 minutes, or until tender, turning the vegetables halfway through the cooking.

Steamin' Vegetable Medley

6 to 8 servings

Just like a musical medley, this dish offers you a variety, too. It's a variety of vegetable tastes. I know your gang is going to sing praises to the cook . . . and that'll be *you!*

½ cup water
5 medium-sized carrots, peeled
    and cut into ¼-inch slices
3 medium-sized zucchini, cut into
    ¼-inch slices
3 medium-sized yellow squash,
    cut into ¼-inch slices

2 tablespoons butter
1 teaspoon dried dillweed
½ teaspoon onion powder
¼ teaspoon garlic powder
½ teaspoon salt

In a large skillet, bring the water to a boil over medium-high heat. Add the carrots, cover, and cook for 3 to 4 minutes. Add the zucchini and yellow squash and cook, uncovered, for 5 minutes, or until the water evaporates. Reduce the heat to low and add the remaining ingredients; stir until well combined. Cook for 5 to 8 minutes, or until the vegetables are tender.

Honey Stir-fry Vegetables

4 to 6 servings

Stir-fry without oil?! Yup! And the sauce is loaded with flavor . . . not fat!

6 garlic cloves, crushed
¼ cup honey
1 tablespoon light soy sauce
1 tablespoon cornstarch
1 teaspoon sesame seeds
½ cup ready-to-use vegetable
    broth

1 pound wax beans, trimmed
⅓ pound snow peas, trimmed
1 large red bell pepper, cut into
    ¼-inch strips

In a small bowl, combine the garlic, honey, soy sauce, and cornstarch; mix well and set aside. In a large skillet or wok, cook the sesame seeds over medium-high heat for 2 to 3 minutes, until golden. Add the broth and wax beans; cook for 5 minutes, stirring occasionally. Add the snow peas and red peppers and cook for 2 minutes, stirring constantly. Add the honey mixture; mix well. Cook for 2 minutes, or until the sauce thickens, stirring occasionally.

New England Baked Beans

6 to 9 servings

I love New England, especially the food! So I found a great way to enjoy their fabulous baked beans right at home. They're as close as my—or your—cupboard and oven!

1 can (15 to 19 ounces) red kidney beans, rinsed and drained
1 can (15 to 19 ounces) cannellini beans (white kidney beans), rinsed and drained

1 medium-sized onion, chopped
1 jar (12 ounces) chili sauce
½ cup ketchup
2 tablespoons firmly packed dark brown sugar
2 teaspoons dry mustard

Preheat the oven to 325°F. Combine all the ingredients in a large bowl. Pour into an 8-inch square baking dish that has been coated with nonstick vegetable spray. Bake for 50 to 60 minutes, or until the sauce is bubbly and thickened.

Corn Bake-off

3 to 4 servings

If you're going to a potluck dinner, or if you just need something delicious and quick to put on the table for your hungry gang, here's one that's really simple to make. And the Mexican-style corn gives it a zesty tang that'll make them think you slaved in the kitchen for them!

1 can (11 ounces) Mexican-style corn, drained
1 can (15 ounces) cream-style corn
¼ cup dry bread crumbs

1 egg
2 egg whites
½ teaspoon salt
⅛ teaspoon black pepper
Nonstick vegetable spray

Preheat the oven to 350°F. Combine all the ingredients except the vegetable spray in a medium-sized bowl; mix well. Pour into an 8-inch square baking dish that has been coated with nonstick vegetable spray. Coat the top with vegetable spray and bake for 45 to 50 minutes, or until golden.

Cheesy Cauliflower and Broccoli

4 to 6 servings

I'll admit that this isn't a nonfat recipe, but I adapted one of my favorite veggie dishes and was able to cut the fat and calories almost in half. Now I've got a new, lighter favorite!

1 package (10 ounces) frozen
    cauliflower
1 package (10 ounces) frozen
    broccoli
1 can (10¾ ounces) reduced-fat
    condensed cream of
    mushroom soup

¼ cup low-fat milk
¼ cup grated Parmesan cheese
½ cup (2 ounces) shredded part-
    skim mozzarella cheese

Cook the vegetables according to the package directions; drain and set aside. In a medium-sized saucepan, combine the soup, milk, and Parmesan cheese over medium heat. Cook for 5 to 6 minutes, until heated through and bubbly. Add the mozzarella cheese and stir until melted. Add the cooked vegetables and toss to coat; stir until heated through.

NOTE: Served with a grilled chicken breast and a baked potato . . . wow, what a meal!

Crunchy Baked Green Beans

4 to 6 servings

Here's a 40-year-old favorite with a new turn. Reduced-fat soup adds the flavor we need. And water chestnuts now add the crunch.

1 package (16 ounces) frozen
   green beans, thawed
1 can (10¾ ounces) reduced-fat
   condensed cream of
   mushroom soup

1 can (8 ounces) sliced water
   chestnuts, drained

Preheat the oven to 350°F. Combine all the ingredients in a large bowl; mix well. Spoon into a 7" × 11" baking dish that has been coated with nonstick vegetable spray. Bake for 35 to 40 minutes, or until the beans are tender and heated through.

NOTE: For an extra flavor accent, sprinkle a tablespoon of grated Parmesan cheese over the top before serving.

Roasted Tomatoes

4 to 8 servings (see Note)

When our gardens reward us with a generous supply of tomatoes, here's a different way to enjoy them.

4 medium-sized tomatoes
2 tablespoons olive oil
¼ teaspoon garlic powder

¼ teaspoon onion powder
¼ teaspoon salt
¼ teaspoon black pepper

Preheat the oven to 450°F. Core the tomatoes, cut them in half, and gently squeeze out some of the juices. Combine the remaining ingredients in a small bowl. Rub the mixture onto the cut surfaces of the tomatoes and place them cut side up in a 9" × 13" baking dish. Bake for 20 to 25 minutes, until soft but not mushy.

NOTE: Why not add ¼ teaspoon of dried dillweed, basil, or oregano, too? Use my recipe as a starting point and make these your own, as a side dish or for adding to cooked pasta or rice. So, depending on how you use them, the yield really will vary.

Sweet-and-Sour Red Cabbage

6 to 8 servings

Serve it up hot or cold with poultry or a hearty slow-cooked roast.

1 small head red cabbage, shredded	½ cup apple cider vinegar
1 medium-sized onion, chopped	½ cup sugar
1 cup water	¼ teaspoon ground cloves
	½ teaspoon salt

Combine all the ingredients in a large saucepan and bring to a boil over medium-high heat. Reduce the heat to low, cover, and simmer for 40 to 45 minutes, or until the cabbage is tender.

NOTE: This will last in the fridge, covered, for a week or two. Oh, I recommend storing it in a glass container because plastic containers would probably be stained by the red cabbage, and metal ones may react with the vinegar, giving it a metallic taste.

Spicy Polenta Pancakes

5 to 6 servings

I was first introduced to these at a county fair in the South, but I had them straight from the deep fryer. Sure, they tasted good, but watching what we eat is now as important as how good things taste. And the best part is that I don't feel cheated with this all-new version!

1 can (4 ounces) chopped green chilies, drained	½ cup reduced-fat sour cream
¾ cup low-fat milk	1 egg white
¾ cup all-purpose flour	1 tablespoon sugar
½ cup yellow cornmeal	¾ teaspoon baking soda
	½ teaspoon baking powder

In a large bowl, combine all the ingredients; mix well. Coat a medium-sized skillet or griddle with nonstick vegetable spray, then heat over medium heat until a drop of water sizzles on the surface. Pour 2 tablespoons of the batter onto the griddle for each pancake, making 3-inch circles. Cook for 2 to 3 minutes, until bubbles begin to form on the top and the surface has a dry appearance. Flip the pancakes and cook for 1 to 2 more minutes, or until golden brown on both sides.

NOTE: With 3 or 4 pancakes topped with some picante sauce or additional reduced-fat sour cream on a dinner plate and Fast Chicken Fajitas (page 107), you've got a complete meal.

Breads and Muffins

I used to love to sit down at the table and go right for the bread basket. And when the breads, rolls, and muffins were warm, it was heavenly. I still enjoy the bread basket, but I exercise much better control now. Here are some of my tricks:

- Try eating breads and baked goods that are lower in fat, such as bagels, pitas, tortillas, and English muffins instead of croissants and breakfast Danish.
- Make or buy smaller-sized baked goods, like miniature dinner rolls and thin-sliced breads. Reducing serving sizes cuts down on calories and fat (unless you consume a larger quantity, defeating the purpose totally!).
- When baking breads or muffins, use egg whites in place of whole eggs whenever possible. (Two egg whites equal one whole egg.)
- To reduce baked-in calories and fat, start with items that are lower in fat, such as skim milk and reduced-fat sour cream and cream cheese.
- Applesauce and prune purée are good alternatives to oil in baking. Substitute for either some or the entire amount of oil called for in a recipe.
- Use dried fruit instead of nuts and chocolate chips whenever possible. If you do choose to include nuts or chocolate chips, cut back on the amount and use miniature chips. (They go a long way.)
- If you're looking for something to spread on your breads and muffins, use an-ever-so-thin layer of butter or margarine, or alternatives like jam, jelly, apple butter, or reduced-fat butter or cream cheese.

Breads and Muffins

Lighter Onion Bread

I loaf

No kneading or proofing dough. Just mixing, baking, cooling, and eating! The trick is in the biscuit baking mix.

1 tablespoon butter
1 large onion, finely chopped
3 cups reduced-fat biscuit
    baking mix

1 egg
1 cup low-fat milk
1 teaspoon dried basil
1 teaspoon dried dillweed

Preheat the oven to 350°F. In a large skillet over medium heat, melt the butter and sauté the onion for 5 to 7 minutes, or until lightly golden. In a large bowl, combine the remaining ingredients. Add the sautéed onion to the biscuit mixture; stir just until blended. Spoon the mixture into a 9" × 5" loaf pan that has been coated with nonstick baking spray. Bake for 55 to 60 minutes, or until golden on top. Allow to cool before removing from the pan.

Chili Corn Bread

9 squares

Isn't it about time for a change from traditional types of breads? This one's so zippy that you'll forget it's "a little lighter."

1⅓ cups self-rising cornmeal mix (see Note)
1 can (8¾ ounces) whole kernel corn, drained
2 tablespoons minced scallions

1 teaspoon chili powder
1 can (4 ounces) chopped green chilies, drained
3 egg whites
½ cup low-fat milk

Preheat the oven to 350°F. In a large bowl, combine the cornmeal, corn, scallions, and chili powder. Stir in the chilies, egg whites, and milk just until moistened. Do not overmix. Pour the batter into an 8-inch square baking dish that has been coated with nonstick baking spray. Bake for 25 to 30 minutes, or until a wooden toothpick inserted in the center comes out clean.

NOTE: Self-rising cornmeal mix is found along with the flours in the supermarket. Don't substitute plain cornmeal for it, 'cause it won't work the same way.

Tangy Bread Sticks

16 bread sticks

There's no need to spread these with butter, 'cause the richness is baked right in. And if you'd like a low-fat dipping option, why not warm up some spicy marinara sauce to serve with 'em?

2¼ to 2⅔ cups all-purpose flour
1 package (¼ ounce) active dry
    yeast
1 teaspoon dried oregano
1 teaspoon salt
1 cup warm water

1 teaspoon sugar
½ teaspoon hot pepper sauce
1 tablespoon olive oil, divided
1 tablespoon caraway seeds
1 teaspoon coarse (kosher) salt

Place 2¼ cups flour, the yeast, oregano, and salt in a food processor that has been fitted with its steel cutting blade. Pulse for 3 to 5 seconds, or until the ingredients are well mixed. In a small bowl, combine the water, sugar, hot pepper sauce, and 2 teaspoons oil. With the processor running, slowly pour the water mixture through the feeding tube. If the dough is too soft, add the remaining flour 1 tablespoon at a time until it forms a smooth ball. Add the caraway seeds and process for 20 seconds. Place the dough in a bowl that has been coated with nonstick baking spray and cover with plastic wrap; turn to coat. Let rise for 35 to 40 minutes, or until doubled in size. Preheat the oven to 450°F. Divide the dough into 16 pieces and shape each piece into a ball. With lightly floured hands, roll each ball into a rope about 12 inches long. Lay 2 inches apart on 2 cookie sheets that have been coated with nonstick baking spray. Brush the remaining 1 teaspoon oil over the bread sticks and sprinkle with the coarse salt. Bake for 10 to 12 minutes, or until golden brown.

Apple Flat Bread

24 to 30 slices

How 'bout serving bread for dessert? You can with this one. And with a scoop of frozen low-fat vanilla yogurt, it's really super.

1 pound store-bought pizza dough
¼ cup apple jelly, melted
4 medium-sized apples, cored,
    peeled, and sliced

1 tablespoon sugar
2 teaspoons ground cinnamon

Preheat the oven to 350°F. On a lightly floured surface, roll out the dough to a 10" × 15" rectangle and place on a rimmed baking sheet that has been coated with nonstick baking spray. With your fingertips, gently spread the dough to cover the pan, and push it up to the edges of the pan, forming a rim. If the dough is too sticky, dust it and your hands lightly with flour. Spread the apple jelly over the dough, then top with the sliced apples, arranged in a single layer. In a small bowl, combine the sugar and cinnamon. Sprinkle over the apples. Bake for 17 to 20 minutes, or until the edges are golden. Remove from the oven and cool slightly in the pan on a wire rack. Slice and serve warm.

NOTE: If you want to make this favorite all through the year, fresh sliced peaches, or whatever is in season, will work, too. So will prunes and other dried fruit.

Cranberry Nut Scones

8 scones

These are English scones with a twist . . . one that deserves to be noticed. And when you serve these, I guarantee they'll be noticed!

2 cups all-purpose flour
¼ cup plus 1 teaspoon sugar, divided
1 tablespoon baking powder
¼ teaspoon salt
¼ cup (½ stick) room-temperature butter, cut into 4 even slices

⅓ cup sweetened dried cranberries
⅓ cup coarsely chopped walnuts
1 can (5.33 ounces) evaporated skim milk
1 egg

Preheat the oven to 400°F. In a medium-sized bowl, combine the flour, ¼ cup sugar, the baking powder, and salt; mix well. Cut the butter into the flour mixture until crumbly, then stir in the cranberries and walnuts. In a small bowl, combine the milk and egg; whisk to mix. Add the egg mixture to the flour and stir just until blended. On a floured surface, knead the dough 5 to 6 times, then place on an ungreased baking sheet and press into a circle about 1 inch thick and 8 inches across. Cut into 8 wedges, but do not separate. Sprinkle with the remaining 1 teaspoon sugar. Bake on the middle oven rack for 18 to 22 minutes, or until golden brown.

NOTE: Sweetened dried cranberries are becoming widely available and make a super snack or mix-in.

Cape Cod Cranberry Loaf

1 loaf

Did you know that more cranberries are produced on Cape Cod than anywhere else in the country? And that's just where the original version of this recipe came from.

¼ cup egg substitute
¼ cup sunflower or vegetable oil
1 cup sugar
¾ cup orange juice
½ cup walnuts
1 cup fresh or frozen cranberries,
    thawed

2 cups all-purpose flour
1½ teaspoons baking powder
½ teaspoon baking soda
1 teaspoon salt

Preheat the oven to 350°F. In a food processor that has been fitted with its steel cutting blade, combine the egg substitute, oil, sugar, orange juice, walnuts, and cranberries. Pulse until the nuts and cranberries are coarsely chopped. In a medium-sized bowl, combine the flour, baking powder, baking soda, and salt. Add the cranberry mixture and stir just until the mixture is moistened and blended. Pour the batter into a 9" × 5" loaf pan that has been coated with nonstick baking spray and bake for 50 to 60 minutes, or until lightly browned on top and a wooden toothpick inserted in the center comes out clean. Cool in the pan on a wire rack.

Cola Date Loaf

I loaf

Make this and see if your gang can guess the secret ingredient that gives it so much flavor. Of course, you can't tell them the name first—that'll give it away!

1 can (12 ounces) diet cola beverage

1 package (8 ounces) pitted dates, coarsely chopped

1 cup firmly packed light brown sugar

2 tablespoons vegetable oil

2 cups all-purpose flour

1 teaspoon baking soda

1 teaspoon baking powder

1 teaspoon ground cinnamon

1 egg

1 teaspoon vanilla extract

Preheat the oven to 350°F. Place the cola in a medium-sized saucepan and bring to a boil over medium-high heat. Remove from the heat and stir in the dates, brown sugar, and oil, mixing well. Set aside to cool. In a medium-sized bowl, combine the flour, baking soda, baking powder, and cinnamon; stir to mix well. Add the flour mixture to the cola mixture, then stir in the egg and vanilla extract until well blended. Spoon the batter into a 9" × 5" loaf pan that has been coated with nonstick baking spray. Bake for 55 to 60 minutes, or until a wooden toothpick inserted in the center comes out clean. Cool on a wire rack for 15 minutes before removing from the pan.

Lemon Poppy Seed Bread

1 loaf

Please don't let the list of ingredients intimidate you. If you don't already have everything on hand, none of it's hard to get. And, believe me, it's a nice treat for your family and friends.

¼ cup (½ stick) butter, softened
¼ cup applesauce
1 cup granulated sugar
½ cup egg substitute
1½ cups all-purpose flour
1 teaspoon baking powder

½ teaspoon salt
½ cup low-fat milk
1 tablespoon grated lemon zest
1 teaspoon poppy seeds
3 tablespoons lemon juice
¼ cup confectioners' sugar

Preheat the oven to 350°F. In a medium-sized bowl, with an electric beater on medium speed, beat the butter, applesauce, granulated sugar, and egg substitute until smooth. In another medium-sized bowl, combine the flour, baking powder, and salt. Add the flour mixture to the applesauce mixture, beating until well combined. Add the milk, lemon zest, and poppy seeds. Pour the batter into a 9" × 5" loaf pan that has been coated with nonstick baking spray. Bake for 45 to 50 minutes, or until a wooden toothpick inserted in the center comes out clean. In a small bowl, combine the lemon juice and confectioners' sugar, stirring until smooth and creamy. Pour over the loaf when it comes out of the oven, then allow to cool in the pan.

Saucy Banana Bread

I loaf

Give overripe bananas a yummy new life. And in this recipe, applesauce takes the place of butter—so our all-time favorite is now better than ever in more ways than one!

1 cup sugar
¾ cup applesauce
2 eggs
2 cups all-purpose flour
1 teaspoon baking soda

½ teaspoon salt
1 cup mashed ripe bananas
   (about 3 medium-sized
   bananas)
1 teaspoon vanilla extract

Preheat the oven to 350°F. In a large bowl, cream together the sugar and applesauce with an electric beater on medium-high speed. Add the eggs and beat thoroughly. Gradually add the flour, baking soda, and salt, blending to mix well. Beat in the mashed bananas and vanilla extract until well mixed. Pour the batter into a 9" × 5" loaf pan that has been coated with nonstick baking spray. Bake for 55 to 60 minutes, or until light golden brown. Immediately remove from the pan and place on a wire rack to cool.

NOTE: Shop for bananas that are very ripe and turning brown. They're the ones that are usually on sale *and* that give this the best flavor. What a deal! For banana muffins, just coat a 12-cup muffin pan with nonstick baking spray, fill the muffin cups ¾-full with batter, and bake for 17 to 20 minutes, or until light golden.

Zucchini Bread

I loaf

What a great way to get more vegetables into our diets. Five portions of fruits and veggies a day? No problem (especially when they taste this good)!

1 egg
2 egg whites
½ cup applesauce
½ cup vegetable oil
1 cup sugar
2 teaspoons vanilla extract
2½ cups all-purpose flour

1 teaspoon baking soda
½ teaspoon baking powder
2 teaspoons ground cinnamon
1 teaspoon salt
2 cups shredded zucchini
1 cup raisins

Preheat the oven to 350°F. In a large bowl, with an electric beater on medium speed, beat the egg and egg whites until fluffy. Add the applesauce, oil, sugar, and vanilla. Continue beating for 2 to 3 minutes, or until well blended. In a medium-sized bowl, combine the flour, baking soda, baking powder, cinnamon, and salt. Gradually add the flour mixture to the egg mixture and beat just until blended. With a spoon, stir in the zucchini and raisins. Pour the mixture into a 9" × 5" loaf pan that has been coated with nonstick baking spray. Bake for 75 to 80 minutes, or until a wooden toothpick inserted in the center comes out clean. Remove from the pan and cool on a wire rack.

Applesauce Bread

1 loaf

Here's a goodie where I've been able to replace all-purpose flour with whole wheat flour to help us enjoy getting some extra fiber. It's got a full, nutty taste and texture I think you'll like.

2 cups whole wheat flour
1 teaspoon baking soda
½ teaspoon baking powder
1 teaspoon ground cinnamon
½ teaspoon ground nutmeg

1½ cups applesauce
⅔ cup sugar
2 tablespoons vegetable oil
2 egg whites
¼ cup low-fat milk

Preheat the oven to 350°F. In a medium-sized bowl, combine the flour, baking soda, baking powder, cinnamon, and nutmeg. In a large bowl, combine the applesauce, sugar, vegetable oil, egg whites, and milk; mix well. Gradually add the flour mixture and mix until blended. Pour into a 9" × 5" loaf pan that has been coated with nonstick baking spray. Bake for 55 to 60 minutes, or until a wooden toothpick inserted in the center comes out clean. Remove from the pan and cool on a wire rack.

NOTE: You can even bake this batter in a 12-cup muffin pan for a high-fiber take-along snack. And the muffins need to bake for only 25 to 35 minutes.

Blueberry-Patch Muffins

12 muffins

I call these Blueberry-Patch Muffins because of their great fresh taste. Now don't worry—they aren't really involved. As a matter of fact, you can be enjoying these muffins right out of the oven in about 30 minutes!

2 cups all-purpose flour
1 tablespoon baking powder
½ cup sugar
½ teaspoon salt
¼ cup egg substitute

1 cup low-fat milk
¼ cup sunflower oil
¼ teaspoon vanilla extract
1 can (16 ounces) blueberries in
   heavy syrup, drained (see
   Note)

Preheat the oven to 375°F. In a large bowl, combine the flour, baking powder, sugar, and salt. Add the remaining ingredients except the blueberries. Stir just until blended. Gently fold in the blueberries. Coat a 12-cup muffin pan with nonstick baking spray. Fill each cup ¾-full with the batter and bake for 20 to 25 minutes, or until the tops are golden brown and spring back when lightly touched.

NOTE: Don't confuse blueberries in heavy syrup with blueberry pie filling—they're different products.

Apple-Walnut Bran Muffins

12 muffins

Who said muffins can't be a little lighter yet still be packed with great taste? Maybe you should make a double batch of these, 'cause they freeze well (if there are any left after they hit your table!).

1 cup toasted wheat bran
1 cup all-purpose flour
1½ teaspoons baking soda
1 teaspoon baking powder
½ teaspoon salt
¼ cup chopped walnuts
¾ cup low-fat plain yogurt

½ cup firmly packed light brown
    sugar
⅓ cup applesauce
¼ cup egg substitute
2 tablespoons molasses
1 medium-sized apple, peeled,
    cored, and chopped

Preheat the oven to 400°F. In a large bowl, combine the wheat bran, flour, baking soda, baking powder, salt, and walnuts. In a medium-sized bowl, combine the yogurt, brown sugar, applesauce, egg substitute, and molasses; stir until well mixed. Add the yogurt mixture to the wheat bran mixture and stir just until blended. Gently fold in the apple. Coat a 12-cup muffin pan with nonstick baking spray. Fill each cup ¾-full with the batter and bake for 15 to 20 minutes, or until the tops are golden brown and spring back when lightly touched.

NOTE: Oh, by the way, don't think that by calling for toasted wheat bran I mean for you to put wheat bran in your toaster! Toasted wheat bran can be found just that way (already toasted) in the supermarket cereal aisle.

Sunshine Muffins

12 muffins

Bring something "light and bright" to your table. With orange marmalade swirled into a basic muffin batter, these are a perfect breakfast or brunch go-along.

1 whole egg
2 egg whites
¼ cup sugar
1¾ cups all-purpose flour
2 teaspoons baking powder

½ teaspoon salt
¾ cup low-fat milk
2 tablespoons butter, melted
1 teaspoon vanilla extract
½ cup orange marmalade

Preheat the oven to 400°F. In a large bowl, with an electric beater on medium speed, beat the whole egg and egg whites until fluffy. Add the sugar and beat until creamy. With a spoon, stir in the flour, baking powder, and salt. Add the milk, butter, and vanilla; mix until well combined, then stir in the marmalade. Coat a 12-cup muffin pan with nonstick baking spray. Fill each cup ⅔-full with batter and bake for 20 to 25 minutes, or until a wooden toothpick inserted in the center comes out clean.

Oat Bran Flapjacks

About 16 pancakes

When our kids were little, we went camping as many weekends as we could during the summers. We all loved our Sunday morning pancakes (we called them flapjacks) made over the fire in our cast-iron skillet. I've tried to re-create that goodness with these. Bring back any memories for *you*?

1½ cups all-purpose flour
¾ cup quick-cooking or old-
    fashioned rolled oats
½ cup oat bran
1 teaspoon baking powder

1 teaspoon ground cinnamon
⅔ cup maple syrup
½ cup egg substitute
1 cup low-fat milk

In a medium-sized bowl, combine the flour, oats, oat bran, baking powder, and cinnamon. Stir in the syrup, egg substitute, and milk just until moistened. Coat a large skillet with nonstick vegetable spray and heat over medium heat until a drop of water sizzles when dropped on the surface. Reduce the heat to medium-low and drop 2 tablespoonfuls of batter onto the skillet to form each pancake. Cook for 2 to 3 minutes, or until lightly browned on the bottom, then flip over to brown the other side. Repeat until all of the batter is used.

Desserts

When I first started watching what I ate, my family and friends were really surprised when they saw me making and eating desserts. Know why? Almost all of them had been on diets before that had prohibited them from eating desserts. So, they cheated. Well, I didn't want any part of that!

I've put together a whole chapter for you that's packed with desserts that taste good even though they're a little lighter. There's Old-fashioned Bread Pudding (page 307) and Little Italy Cheese-cake (page 294) . . . and even Blueberry Cobbler (page 300) and Lemon Pound Cake (page 299). As I said in my Introduction, I've cut down on fat in many of these recipes. There's also less sugar in some, and fewer eggs in others.

And here are a few tricks you can use to cut out the guilt when making your own homemade favorites:

- Fresh fruit and fruit compotes make great desserts.
- Enjoy lower-fat ice cream, ice milk, frozen yogurt, and ices instead of regular ice cream as a refreshing, always-available dessert.
- In many recipes, egg whites can substitute for whole eggs. Do your own experimenting. (Two egg whites equal one whole egg.)
- Top desserts with reduced-fat whipped topping. And I don't know about you, but I like to top pudding and flavored gelatins with a little skim milk or sweetened yogurt instead of heavier alternatives.
- Top frozen yogurt and low-fat ice cream with a bit of jam or

fruit preserves. And check out all the low-fat dessert topping alternatives there are in the stores now.

- It's possible to enjoy cheesecake and other rich desserts by using reduced-fat cream cheese, ricotta cheese, and sour cream.
- I found a great low-fat trick for holding crumb crusts together by using jelly or marmalade! See pages 293 and 296.
- If buying store-bought goodies, read the labels carefully. A lot of times the amount of fat is low while the sugar content is extremely high. It's important to watch fat *and* calories.

By following these rules and using common sense, you can get a lighter "OOH IT'S SO GOOD!!®"

Desserts

Bite-Sized Chocolate Chippers

About 5 dozen cookies

Chocolate chip cookies—in a lighter book? Sure! By using egg whites instead of whole eggs, and cutting the usual amount of butter and chips in half, you'll simply lose calories, not goodness. (That is, of course, unless you eat more than your fair share . . . so, watch it!)

3 cups all-purpose flour
1½ teaspoons baking soda
½ teaspoon salt
1¼ cups firmly packed light
   brown sugar
½ cup granulated sugar

½ cup (1 stick) butter, softened
1 teaspoon vanilla extract
2 egg whites
⅓ cup water
1 cup miniature semisweet
   chocolate chips

Preheat the oven to 350°F. In a medium-sized bowl, combine the flour, baking soda, and salt; set aside. In a large bowl, cream together the brown sugar, granulated sugar, butter, and vanilla; beat in the egg whites. Gradually beat in the flour mixture alternately with the water. Stir in the chocolate chips. Drop by teaspoonfuls about 1 inch apart onto cookie sheets that have been coated with nonstick baking spray; bake for 12 to 14 minutes, or until lightly golden. Let stand for 2 minutes, then remove to a wire rack to cool completely.

Chewy Peanut Butter Cookies

About 2 dozen cookies

It's hard to believe that peanut butter has been lightened up. Well, it has, so why not take advantage of it?!

1 cup sugar
1 cup low-fat creamy peanut
   butter

¼ cup egg substitute
1 teaspoon vanilla extract

Preheat the oven to 325°F. In a medium-sized bowl, combine all the ingredients until thoroughly mixed. Drop by teaspoonfuls about 1 inch apart onto nonstick cookie sheets. Press a crisscross pattern into the top of each cookie with the tines of a fork. Bake for 10 minutes, or until light golden. Cool before removing from the pan.

NOTE: Not your average peanut butter cookies, these are *really* chewy.

Oatmeal Chocolate Chip Cookies

About 4 dozen cookies

Get the best of both worlds with chocolate chip cookies and oatmeal cookies all rolled (actually dropped!) into one.

1¾ cups all-purpose flour
1 teaspoon baking soda
½ teaspoon salt
1¼ cups firmly packed light brown sugar
½ cup granulated sugar
½ cup (1 stick) butter, softened

½ cup unsweetened applesauce
2 egg whites
1 tablespoon vanilla extract
2½ cups quick-cooking or old-fashioned rolled oats
½ cup miniature semisweet chocolate chips

Preheat the oven to 375°F. In a small bowl, combine the flour, baking soda, and salt; set aside. In a large bowl, with an electric beater on medium speed, beat the brown sugar, granulated sugar, butter, and applesauce until smooth. Beat in the egg whites and vanilla. Gradually beat in the flour mixture until smooth. With a spoon, stir in the oats and chocolate chips. Drop by rounded teaspoonfuls 2 to 3 inches apart onto cookie sheets that have been coated with nonstick baking spray. Bake for 9 to 11 minutes, or until golden. Cool on the pans for 2 minutes, then remove to a wire rack to cool completely.

Shortcut Brownies

12 to 15 squares

By using prepared brownie mix, applesauce, and egg whites, you get to lighten up the calories while lightening up your work, too!

1 package (21 to 23 ounces)
    brownie mix
½ cup plus 1 teaspoon
    applesauce, divided
¼ cup water

3 egg whites
¼ cup quick-cooking or
    old-fashioned rolled oats
2 tablespoons light brown sugar

Preheat the oven to 350°F. In a large bowl, combine the brownie mix, ½ cup applesauce, the water, and egg whites; stir with a spoon until thoroughly mixed. Pour into a 9" × 13" baking dish that has been coated with nonstick baking spray. In a small bowl, combine the remaining 1 teaspoon applesauce, the oats, and brown sugar; mix with a fork until crumbly. Sprinkle over the brownie batter and bake for 25 to 28 minutes, or until a wooden toothpick inserted in the center comes out clean. Cool, then cut into bars.

Low-Fat Fudgy Brownies

9 to 12 squares

Did you know that in most dark baked goods you can replace the fat with prune purée? Yup! And it's found right in your supermarket baking department.

4 ounces unsweetened chocolate, cut into 1-inch pieces
3 egg whites
1 cup sugar
½ cup prune purée or prepared prune butter

1 teaspoon salt
1 teaspoon vanilla extract
½ cup all-purpose flour
¼ cup chopped walnuts (optional)

Preheat the oven to 350°F. Heat the chocolate in a double boiler, in the microwave, or on the stove in a saucepan over low heat, stirring occasionally, just until melted. (Do not allow to boil.) Transfer to a large bowl; add the remaining ingredients except the flour and nuts, and stir until well combined. Stir in the flour. Spread the batter in an 8-inch square baking dish that has been coated with nonstick baking spray; sprinkle with the nuts, if desired. Bake for 25 to 30 minutes, or until a wooden toothpick inserted in the center comes out clean. Cool in the pan on a wire rack; cut into squares when cool.

NOTE: You can make your own prune purée by combining 4 ounces pitted prunes with 3 tablespoons water in a food processor. Pulse until the mixture is smooth, making about ½ cup.

Chewy Apple Raisin Bars

15 to 20 bars

Super, simple, and satisfying. I have no choice! That's how I have to describe these.

1 cup all-purpose flour
1 cup sugar
¼ teaspoon baking powder
½ teaspoon salt
2 eggs, beaten

1 medium-sized apple, peeled,
    cored, and finely chopped
1 cup raisins
¼ cup applesauce

Preheat the oven to 350°F. In a large bowl, combine the flour, sugar, baking powder, and salt. Add the remaining ingredients; mix well. Spread the batter in a 9" × 13" baking dish that has been coated with nonstick baking spray and bake for 40 to 50 minutes, or until the edges are golden. Cut into bars while still warm.

Frozen Orchard Pie

8 to 10 servings

If you're like me and often get cravings for ice cream, but want to keep your sweet intake in check, don't fret! The answer is as easy as pie.

1½ cups finely crushed
    gingersnaps
⅓ cup orange marmalade

1 quart butter pecan or vanilla
    frozen yogurt, softened
1 cup apple butter

In a medium-sized bowl, combine the crushed gingersnaps and orange marmalade; mix well. Spread evenly over the bottom and up the sides of a 9-inch pie plate that has been coated with nonstick baking spray, forming a firm crust. In a large bowl, combine the softened frozen yogurt and the apple butter until well blended; spoon the mixture evenly into the pie crust. Cover and freeze for at least 3 to 4 hours, or until firm. Remove from the freezer and allow to sit for 15 minutes before serving.

Cranberry Pineapple Freeze

Here's a whole new way with frozen dessert. Is it fruit muffins or smooth, fruity ice cream? Whatever you want it to be, you're gonna love it.

1 package (8 ounces) reduced-fat
    cream cheese
1 cup reduced-fat sour cream
¾ cup sugar

1 cup whole-berry cranberry
    sauce
1 can (8 ounces) crushed
    pineapple, drained

In a medium-sized bowl, with an electric beater on medium speed, beat the cream cheese, sour cream, and sugar until smooth. With a spoon, gently stir in the cranberry sauce and pineapple. Line a 12-cup muffin pan with paper or foil liners and divide the mixture evenly among them. Cover and freeze for 3 hours, or until firm.

Apple Cream Pie

8 servings

Watch their faces when you bring this to the table and tell them you're watching what you serve.

1 package (8 ounces) reduced-fat cream cheese, softened
1½ cups cold low-fat milk
2 packages (4-serving size) instant vanilla pudding and pie filling mix

1 teaspoon ground cinnamon, divided
One 9-inch prepared reduced-fat graham cracker pie crust
1 can (21 ounces) apple pie filling

Place the cream cheese in a large bowl; with a wire whisk or an electric beater, gradually beat in the milk until smooth. Add the pudding mix and ½ teaspoon cinnamon. Beat for 1 to 2 more minutes, then spread evenly in the pie crust. In a medium-sized bowl, mix the apple pie filling and the remaining ½ teaspoon cinnamon. Spread evenly over the pudding mixture. Cover and chill for 4 hours, or until set. Store any leftover pie in the refrigerator.

Zesty Lemon Meringue Pie

6 to 8 servings

Pucker up! You're in for a treat your taste buds won't forget!

One 9-inch frozen ready-to-bake pie shell, thawed, baked, and cooled
2 cups low-fat milk
¼ cup cornstarch

¾ cup sugar, divided
3 tablespoons lemon juice
Grated zest of 1 large lemon
¼ cup low-fat lemon yogurt
2 egg whites

Prepare the pie shell. In a medium-sized saucepan, combine the milk, cornstarch, and ½ cup sugar over medium heat, stirring constantly until thickened; remove from the heat. Stir in the lemon juice, lemon zest, and lemon yogurt; mix well. Pour into the baked pie shell and refrigerate for 30 minutes. Preheat the oven to 425°F. In a medium-sized bowl, with an electric beater on medium speed, beat the egg whites and the remaining ¼ cup sugar until stiff peaks form. Spread over the top of the chilled pie filling, to the edges of the crust, and bake for 4 to 5 minutes, or until lightly browned on top. Chill for at least 3 hours before serving.

NOTE: Meringues work best on days that aren't too humid, since humidity causes meringue to weep, making the crust soggy. So save this recipe for a cool, dry day.

Frozen Blueberry Pie

8 to 10 servings

Why not have a light dessert on hand for drop-in company? Just slice, garnish, and serve. Of course, they'll think you fussed all day.

1 cup graham cracker crumbs
3 tablespoons grape jelly
1 jar (7 ounces) marshmallow creme
1 package (8 ounces) reduced-fat cream cheese, softened

1 package (12 ounces) frozen blueberries
1 pint vanilla frozen yogurt, softened

Preheat the oven to 350°F. In a small bowl, combine the graham cracker crumbs and grape jelly. Spread evenly over the bottom of a 10-inch deep-dish pie plate and bake for 7 to 10 minutes, or until golden. Set aside to cool. In a large bowl, with an electric beater on medium speed, combine the marshmallow creme and cream cheese. With a spoon, stir in the frozen blueberries and mix until the cheese mixture is colored blue from the blueberries. Swirl in the frozen yogurt just enough to combine; it should have a marbled effect. Pour into the prepared pie shell and freeze for 4 hours, or overnight. Remove from the freezer and let sit for 5 minutes before serving.

NOTE: Garnish each slice with a few fresh or frozen blueberries. And, if you've got some, add a sprig of fresh mint, too.

Little Italy Cheesecake

10 to 12 servings

We've all got our favorite cheesecake recipes. Well, now you're gonna have another one. It's made with ricotta cheese as well as cream cheese—of course, reduced-fat types of both. So you can enjoy that great Italian flavor once again.

¾ cup graham cracker crumbs
2 tablespoons butter, melted
1 container (15 ounces) part-skim ricotta cheese
1 cup low-fat plain yogurt
¾ cup sugar

2 tablespoons all-purpose flour
2 tablespoons lemon juice
1 package (8 ounces) reduced-fat cream cheese, softened
2 eggs
2½ teaspoons vanilla extract

Preheat the oven to 350°F. In a small bowl, combine the graham cracker crumbs and melted butter; press into the bottom of a 10-inch deep-dish glass pie plate. Bake for 3 to 5 minutes, until lightly browned. Let cool. In a large bowl, with an electric beater on medium speed, combine the ricotta cheese, yogurt, sugar, flour, and lemon juice until smooth; set aside. In another large bowl, with an electric beater on medium speed, beat the cream cheese, eggs, and vanilla until thoroughly combined. Add the ricotta mixture, beating on low speed until well combined. Pour into the pie crust and bake for 60 to 65 minutes, or until the center is nearly set. Cool for 30 to 45 minutes, then refrigerate for 4 to 5 hours, or overnight, before serving.

NOTE: Top with fresh strawberry slices or whole blueberries or raspberries, if desired.

Low-Fat Chocolate Sour Cream Cake

9 to 12 squares

Think that even one dessert serving will put you over your calorie limit for the day—especially a rich-tasting chocolate cake like this one? Count again! You may have some calories left to spare for this creamy chocolate sensation.

1 cup all-purpose flour
1 cup sugar
1 cup reduced-fat sour cream
1 egg

3 tablespoons unsweetened cocoa
1 teaspoon baking soda
¼ teaspoon salt

Preheat the oven to 350°F. Combine all the ingredients in a large bowl; mix with an electric beater until smooth and thoroughly combined. Pour the batter into an 8-inch square baking dish that has been coated with nonstick baking spray. Bake for 30 to 35 minutes, or until a wooden toothpick inserted in the center comes out clean. Cool on a wire rack.

NOTE: If you'd like, when the cake is cool, top it with a sprinkle of confectioners' sugar or a mixture of ground cinnamon and granulated sugar.

Unbelievable Cheesecake Squares

9 to 12 squares

You're not going to believe how I keep this crust together—with orange marmalade! Yup, no butter! And it's sure to keep your family together, too—at least until after dessert.

1½ cups graham cracker crumbs
½ cup orange marmalade, divided
1 container (16 ounces) low-fat cottage cheese
1 package (8 ounces) reduced-fat cream cheese, softened

1 cup sugar, divided
¾ cup egg substitute
1 cup reduced-fat sour cream
1 teaspoon vanilla extract

Preheat the oven to 350°F. In a medium-sized bowl, combine the graham cracker crumbs and ¼ cup marmalade; mix well. With the back of a spoon, press the crumb mixture into the bottom of an 8-inch square baking dish that has been coated with nonstick baking spray. Bake for 6 to 8 minutes, or until lightly browned. Remove from the oven and reduce the heat to 300°F. Meanwhile, in a medium-sized bowl, with an electric beater on medium speed, beat the cottage cheese until smooth and creamy. Add the cream cheese and ¾ cup sugar; beat until smooth and well blended. Add the egg substitute and blend well. With a spoon, swirl in the remaining ¼ cup marmalade. Pour the cheese mixture evenly over the graham cracker crust and bake for 45 minutes. Meanwhile, in a medium-sized bowl, combine the sour cream, vanilla, and the remaining ¼ cup sugar. Pour over the top of the baked pie and bake for 10 minutes longer. Cool completely, then chill for at least 2 hours, or until ready to serve. Cut into squares and serve.

NOTE: Garnish this with fresh fruit for added pizzazz!

Apple-Filled Pound Cake

14 to 16 servings

Let me guess—you want something special for a get-together with friends, but you don't want anything that'll weigh you down, right? This will surely fit the bill. With a cup of good coffee, you've got snack or dessert perfection.

4 cups finely chopped unpeeled
   cooking apples
½ cup orange juice, divided
1½ teaspoons ground cinnamon
1 cup granulated sugar
½ cup applesauce
1 whole egg

2 egg whites
2⅔ cups all-purpose flour
2 teaspoons baking powder
¼ teaspoon salt
¼ cup low-fat milk
2½ teaspoons vanilla extract
2 tablespoons brown sugar

Preheat the oven to 350°F. In a medium-sized bowl, combine the apples, ¼ cup orange juice, and the cinnamon; mix well. In a large bowl, with an electric beater on medium speed, beat the granulated sugar and applesauce for 1 to 2 minutes, or until smooth. Add the whole egg and egg whites and beat well. Slowly add half of the flour, the baking powder, salt, milk, and the remaining ¼ cup orange juice; beat in the remaining flour until the batter is well mixed. Add the vanilla and mix well. Pour half of the batter into a 10-inch Bundt pan that has been coated with nonstick baking spray. Top with half of the apple mixture, then cover with the remaining batter. Cover the batter with the remaining apple mixture and sprinkle with the brown sugar. Bake for 60 to 70 minutes, or until a wooden toothpick inserted in the center comes out clean. Cool on a wire rack for 15 minutes, then remove to a serving platter.

All-in-One Carrot Cake

24 squares

The United States Department of Agriculture says we should eat at least five servings a day of fruits and vegetables. Hey, since this dessert has carrots and applesauce, do you think it qualifies?!

2 cups all-purpose flour
2 cups granulated sugar
1 cup applesauce
½ cup vegetable oil
2 eggs
2 teaspoons baking soda

2 teaspoons ground cinnamon
1 teaspoon salt
3 cups finely grated carrots (about 1 pound)
1 cup raisins

Preheat the oven to 350°F. In a large bowl, with an electric beater on medium speed, combine the flour, sugar, applesauce, oil, eggs, baking soda, cinnamon, and salt; blend until the batter is smooth and thick. With a spoon, stir in the carrots and raisins until thoroughly combined. Pour the batter into a 9" × 13" glass baking dish that has been coated with nonstick baking spray. Bake for 40 to 45 minutes, or until a wooden toothpick inserted in the center comes out clean. Let cool completely before cutting into squares.

NOTE: I've got an awesome icing for you: In a medium-sized bowl, with an electric beater on medium speed, beat 1 cup confectioners' sugar with an 8-ounce package of reduced-fat cream cheese and 1 teaspoon vanilla extract. Spread it over the cooled cake, cut into squares, and serve. To add a fresh carrot look, top the frosting with a touch of freshly grated carrot just before serving.

Lemon Pound Cake

12 to 14 servings

If you're looking at these ingredients and saying, "That's not fat-free!"—you're right. But it's got just half the fat of a traditional pound cake, so you can enjoy your favorite again—still with all the flavor you long for.

1 cup (2 sticks) butter, softened
2 cups sugar
3 eggs
2 teaspoons vanilla extract

3 cups all-purpose flour
1 cup low-fat vanilla yogurt, or
    any flavor you prefer
Grated zest of 2 lemons

Preheat the oven to 350°F. In a large bowl, with an electric beater on medium speed, beat the butter and sugar until creamy. Add the eggs and vanilla and continue beating until smooth. Gradually add the flour and yogurt until well mixed. With a spoon, stir in the lemon zest. Spoon the batter into a 9-inch tube pan that has been coated with nonstick baking spray. Bake for 55 to 60 minutes, or until a wooden toothpick inserted in the center comes out clean. Cool on a wire rack.

NOTE: Sometimes I like to use low-fat raspberry yogurt in place of the vanilla. It gives it a nice look and flavor twist.

Blueberry Cobbler

4 to 6 servings

With canned blueberries, we don't have to wait for summer to enjoy delicious blueberry cobbler. We can enjoy summertime tastes any time of the year!

¼ cup plus 2 tablespoons sugar,
    divided
2 tablespoons butter, softened
1 cup all-purpose flour
⅔ cup low-fat milk

2 teaspoons baking powder
¼ teaspoon salt
1 can (16 ounces) blueberries in
    heavy syrup (*not* pie filling),
    undrained

Preheat the oven to 375°F. In a medium-sized bowl, with an electric beater on medium speed, beat ¼ cup sugar and the butter for about 2 minutes, until creamy. Add the flour, milk, baking powder, and salt and continue beating for 1 to 2 more minutes, or until smooth. Pour the batter into a 9" × 5" baking dish that has been coated with nonstick baking spray. Gently pour the blueberries over the batter, spreading evenly. Sprinkle the remaining 2 tablespoons sugar over the top and bake for 40 to 45 minutes, or until the top is brown and the juices are bubbling.

Steaming Peach Crisp

9 to 12 servings

Watch their eyes light up when you bring this steaming-hot crisp to the table. Just the aroma is enough to bring them running.

¾ cup all-purpose flour, divided
½ cup plus 3 tablespoons light
 brown sugar, divided
1 teaspoon ground cinnamon

3 cans (16 ounces each) sliced
 peaches, drained
Nonstick baking spray

Preheat the oven to 350°F. In a large bowl, combine ¼ cup flour, ½ cup brown sugar, and the cinnamon; mix well. Stir in the peaches until evenly coated. Place in an 8-inch square glass baking dish that has been coated with nonstick baking spray. In a small bowl, combine the remaining ½ cup flour and 3 tablespoons brown sugar; sprinkle over the peach mixture. Spray the top with nonstick baking spray and bake for 25 to 30 minutes, or until the top is lightly browned. Spoon into individual serving dishes.

NOTE: Serve with a scoop of low-fat frozen yogurt or a dollop of light whipped topping.

Raspberry Meringue Spectacular

12 servings

I call it spectacular because that's exactly what it is. They're restaurant-fancy, quick throw-togethers. Now, isn't that what *you* call spectacular?

3 egg whites, at room
　temperature
¼ teaspoon cream of tartar
⅛ teaspoon salt
⅔ cup sugar
½ teaspoon vanilla extract
1 container (12 ounces) light
　frozen whipped topping,
　thawed

¼ cup semisweet chocolate chips,
　finely chopped (see Note)
1 package (12 ounces) frozen
　raspberries, thawed
½ pint fresh raspberries

Preheat the oven to 275°F. Line two 10" × 15" baking sheets with aluminum foil. In a large bowl, with an electric beater on high speed, beat the egg whites, cream of tartar, and salt for 3 to 4 minutes, or until soft peaks form. Gradually add the sugar and beat for 4 to 6 minutes, or until stiff peaks form. Beat in the vanilla. Spoon ¼ cup of the meringue mixture onto the foil, forming a 3-inch mound. Continue with the remaining meringue, making 6 circles on each baking sheet; make sure they do not touch each other. Bake for 1 hour. Turn off the oven and let the meringues sit in the oven for 1 hour. In a medium-sized bowl, fold together the whipped topping, chocolate chips, and thawed raspberries. Spoon over the top of the cooled meringues. Garnish with the fresh raspberries and serve.

NOTE: For best results, process the chocolate chips until finely chopped in a food processor that has been fitted with its steel cutting blade. To prepare these ahead of time, just keep the raspberry chocolate topping refrigerated until ready to serve, then assemble and serve.

Peach Melba Parfaits

5 servings

No, this recipe didn't come from a viewer named Melba. I believe Peach Melba is named for an opera singer. It's raspberry sauce poured over peaches . . . and it's sure a peachy way out of a jam!

1 cup low-fat vanilla yogurt
¼ cup seedless raspberry preserves
    or jam
Half a prepared 9-inch angel food
    cake, cut into ½-inch cubes

1 can (16 ounces) sliced peaches,
    drained and cut into ½-inch
    cubes
½ pint fresh raspberries

In a small bowl, combine the yogurt and raspberry preserves; mix well. Cover the bottom of each of 5 parfait or dessert glasses with a layer of angel food cake. Top with a layer of peaches, then a layer of raspberries. Spoon 2 tablespoons of the yogurt mixture over the fruit, then repeat the layers, using the remaining ingredients. Cover and chill until ready to serve.

NOTE: If fresh raspberries aren't available, you can substitute a cup of thawed and drained frozen raspberries.

Homemade Chocolate Pudding Parfaits

4 servings

Chocolate cravings are enough to drive you crazy sometimes, aren't they? Now you can satisfy the strongest of them with these rich and creamy treats.

½ cup sugar
3 tablespoons cornstarch
2 tablespoons unsweetened cocoa
¼ teaspoon salt

2¼ cups low-fat milk
1 teaspoon vanilla extract
¾ cup crushed vanilla wafers

In a medium-sized saucepan, combine the sugar, cornstarch, cocoa, and salt. Gradually stir in the milk and bring to a boil over medium heat, stirring constantly. Remove from the heat and stir in the vanilla. Allow to cool slightly, then transfer to a large bowl, cover, and chill for 2 hours, or until set. Just before serving, place 1 table-spoon crushed vanilla wafers in each of 4 individual parfait glasses or serving dishes. Top each with ¼ cup of the chocolate pudding. Repeat the layers, then sprinkle the remaining crushed vanilla wafers over the top. Serve immediately.

NOTE: If you'd like, top each serving with a tablespoon of reduced-fat whipped topping.

Raspberry Chocolate Meringue Kisses

About 2 dozen kisses

How could four simple ingredients turn into an award-winning dessert? Here's how. . . .

2 egg whites, at room
    temperature
½ teaspoon vanilla extract
⅓ cup sugar

⅓ cup raspberry-flavored
    semisweet chocolate chips,
    coarsely chopped

Preheat the oven to 325°F. In a large bowl, with an electric beater on medium speed, beat the egg whites and vanilla until soft peaks form. Gradually beat in the sugar until stiff peaks form. With a spoon, fold in the chocolate chips. Drop by tablespoonfuls 2 inches apart onto a cookie sheet that has been coated with nonstick baking spray. Bake for 10 minutes, then turn off the oven. Leave the kisses in the oven for 1 hour. Remove from the oven and cool completely. Store in an airtight container.

NOTE: Regular chocolate chips or miniature chocolate chips can be substituted for the raspberry-flavored chocolate chips.

Old-fashioned Bread Pudding

9 to 12 servings

Bread pudding has been around for years. And if you haven't made it 'cause you thought it was old-fashioned, maybe it's about time to investigate why it's got a taste that never goes out of style.

1 pound day-old bread (10 to 12 slices), torn into 1-inch pieces
2 cups warm water
½ cup raisins
1 egg

2 egg whites
½ cup low-fat milk
1 teaspoon vanilla extract
¾ cup granulated sugar
1 teaspoon salt
½ teaspoon ground cinnamon

Preheat the oven to 350°F. In a large bowl, soak the bread pieces in the water. Stir in the raisins and place in an 8-inch square baking dish that has been coated with nonstick baking spray. In a small bowl, with an electric beater on medium speed, beat the remaining ingredients until well combined. Pour over the bread mixture and bake for 60 to 65 minutes, or until puffy and set in the center. Remove from the oven. Serve immediately.

NOTE: Try topping the pudding with this whiskey glaze: In a small bowl, stir together ½ cup confectioners' sugar and 1 tablespoon plus 2 teaspoons whiskey until smooth. Drizzle over the top of the pudding while still hot from the oven. Serve immediately.

Fluffy Rice Pudding

8 to 10 servings

This yummy rice dessert is so easy, you'll practically be able to make it with your eyes closed. But you'll want to keep them open when you're eating it, so you can get every last bite!

¼ cup (½ stick) butter, softened
½ cup sugar
4 egg whites
3 cups cooked long- or whole-
    grain rice (not instant)

1 cup reduced-fat sour cream
1 cup raisins
½ teaspoon ground cinnamon
½ teaspoon salt

Preheat the oven to 350°F. In a large bowl, with an electric beater on medium speed, cream the butter and sugar until smooth. Beat in the egg whites one at a time. With a spoon, stir in the remaining ingredients; mix well. Pour the mixture into a 1½-quart casserole dish that has been coated with nonstick baking spray. Bake for 45 to 50 minutes, until the center is set. Allow to cool for 10 minutes, then serve while still warm.

Simple Peach Sorbet

3 to 4 servings

You want simple? You've got it! You want low-fat? You've got it! You want delicious, too? Well, guess what—you've got that most of all!

1 can (29 ounces) peaches in
    heavy syrup

1 tablespoon orange juice

Place the unopened can of peaches in the freezer until frozen solid, about 24 hours. Submerge the unopened can in very hot tap water for 1 minute. Open the can and pour any thawed syrup into the bowl of a food processor that has been fitted with its steel cutting blade. Remove the frozen fruit from the can and cut into large chunks; place in the food processor and add the orange juice. Process until smooth, scraping down the sides as needed. Serve immediately, or spoon into an airtight container and freeze until ready to serve.

NOTE: For an even more heavenly flavor, substitute a tablespoon of peach schnapps for the orange juice. You might even want to try making other sorbet flavors by using canned pears and apricots.

Chocolate Sherbet

6 to 8 servings

Your gang is gonna think they're at a fancy restaurant when you open up the freezer and pull out this chocolate concoction. In fact, maybe you'd better make a double batch, 'cause I'd expect them to want seconds.

¾ cup sugar
½ cup unsweetened cocoa
½ cup hot water

2 cups low-fat milk
¼ cup cold water

In a small saucepan, combine the sugar and cocoa. Slowly stir in the hot water and continue stirring over low heat for 2 to 3 minutes, or until the sugar is dissolved and the mixture is warm. Remove from the heat and gradually stir in the milk. Pour into a 9" × 13" baking dish, cover, and freeze for 4 to 6 hours, or until hard. Break up the frozen mixture and place in a blender or a food processor that has been fitted with its steel cutting blade; add the cold water. Blend or process until smooth and light-colored. Pour into an air-tight freezer-proof container; seal and freeze for at least 2 hours, or until set.

Index

Mr. Food®'s Library
Gives You More
Ways to Say. . .
"OOH IT'S SO GOOD!!"®

WILLIAM MORROW

Mr. Food Cooks Like Mama

A

Mr. Food Cooks R·E·A·L AMERICAN
EASY, QUICK, FUN RECIPES
"OOH IT'S SO GOOD!!"

F

THE MR. FOOD COOKBOOK
OOH it's so GOOD!!

B

MR. FOOD COOKS CHICKEN
EASY, QUICK, FUN RECIPES
"OOH IT'S SO GOOD!!"

C

MR. FOOD COOKS PASTA
EASY, QUICK, FUN RECIPES
"OOH IT'S SO GOOD!!"

D

EASY, QUICK, FUN RECIPES
MR. FOOD MAKES DESSERT

E

Mr. Food's Fun Kitchen Tips and Shortcuts (and Recipes, Too!)
"OOH IT'S SO GOOD!!"

J

Mr. Food's FAVORITE COOKIES
"OOH IT'S SO GOOD!!"

G

Quick and Easy Side Dishes

H

Mr. Food Cooks It All in a Snap

I

Old World Cooking Made Easy

K

Mr. Food Simply CHOCOLATE
More than one million copies of Mr. Food cookbooks sold!

O

Mr. Food a little LIGHTER

P

"Help, Mr. Food! Company's Coming"
"OOH IT'S SO GOOD!!"

L

Mr. Food Pizza 1-2-3

M

Mr. Food Meat Around the Table

N

Mr. Food From My Kitchen to Yours:
Stories and Recipes from Home

Q

Mr. Food® CAN HELP YOU BE A KITCHEN HERO!

Let **Mr. Food**® make your life easier with Quick, No-Fuss Recipes and Helpful Kitchen Tips for

Family Dinners • Soups and Salads • Potluck Dishes • Barbecues • Special Brunches • Unbelievable Desserts

. . . and that's just the beginning!

Complete your **Mr. Food**® cookbook library today. It's so simple to share in all the *"OOH IT'S SO GOOD!!®"*

✂ -

TITLE	PRICE	QUANTITY	
A. **Mr. Food**® Cooks Like Mama	@ $14.95 each	x _____	= $_____
B. The **Mr. Food**® Cookbook, *OOH IT'S SO GOOD!!®*	@ $14.95 each	x _____	= $_____
C. **Mr. Food**® Cooks Chicken	@ $11.95 each	x _____	= $_____
D. **Mr. Food**® Cooks Pasta	@ $11.95 each	x _____	= $_____
E. **Mr. Food**® Makes Dessert	@ $11.95 each	x _____	= $_____
F. **Mr. Food**® Cooks Real American	@ $14.95 each	x _____	= $_____
G. **Mr. Food**'s® Favorite Cookies	@ $11.95 each	x _____	= $_____
H. **Mr. Food**'s® Quick and Easy Side Dishes	@ $11.95 each	x _____	= $_____
I. **Mr. Food**® Grills It All in a Snap	@ $11.95 each	x _____	= $_____
J. **Mr. Food**'s® Fun Kitchen Tips and Shortcuts (and Recipes, Too!)	@ $14.95 each	x _____	= $_____
K. **Mr. Food**'s® Old World Cooking Made Easy	@ $14.95 each	x _____	= $_____
L. "Help, **Mr. Food**®! Company's Coming!"	@ $14.95 each	x _____	= $_____
M. **Mr. Food**® Pizza 1-2-3	@ $12.00 each	x _____	= $_____
N. **Mr. Food**® Meat Around the Table	@ $12.00 each	x _____	= $_____
O. **Mr. Food**® Simply Chocolate	@ $12.00 each	x _____	= $_____
P. **Mr. Food**® A Little Lighter	@ $14.95 each	x _____	= $_____
Q. **Mr. Food**® From My Kitchen to Yours: Stories and Recipes from Home	@ $14.95 each	x _____	= $_____
R. **Mr. Food**® Easy Tex-Mex	@ $11.95 each	x _____	= $_____
S. **Mr. Food**® One Pot, One Meal	@ $11.95 each	x _____	= $_____
T. **Mr. Food**® Cool Cravings: Easy Chilled and Frozen Desserts	@ $11.95 each	x _____	= $_____
U. **Mr. Food**'s® Italian Kitchen	@ $14.95 each	x _____	= $_____
V. **Mr. Food**'s® Simple Southern Favorites	@ $14.95 each	x _____	= $_____
W. A **Mr. Food**® Christmas: Homemade and Hassle-Free	@ $19.95 each	x _____	= $_____
X. **Mr. Food**® Cooking by the Calendar	@ $14.95 each	x _____	= $_____
Y. **Mr. Food**'s® Meals in Minutes	@ $14.95 each	x _____	= $_____
Z. **Mr. Food**'s® Good Times, Good Food Cookbook	@ $14.95 each	x _____	= $_____
A A. **Mr. Food**'s® Restaurant Favorites	@ $14.95 each	x _____	= $_____

Send payment to:
Mr. Food®
P.O. Box 9227
Coral Springs, FL 33075-9227

Name _____

Street _____ Apt._____

City _____ State_____ Zip_____
BKS

Method of Payment Enclosed ☐ Check or ☐ Money Order

Please allow up to 6 weeks for delivery.

Book Total	$_____
+ Postage & Handling for *First Copy*	$ **4.00**
+$1 Postage & Handling for Ea. Add'l. Copy (Canadian Orders Add Add'l. $2.00 *Per Copy*)	$_____
Subtotal	$_____
Add 6% Sales Tax (FL Residents Only)	$_____
Total in U.S. Funds	$_____